THE TIMES OF INDIA

THE BEST OF
SPEAKING TREE

VOLUME 4

THE TIMES OF INDIA

THE BEST OF
SPEAKING TREE

VOLUME 4

The Best of Speaking Tree - Volume 4

Copyright ©Bennett, Coleman & Co. Ltd. 2007

Acknowledgements

We thank all those who have contributed to "The Speaking Tree" column in *The Times of India* over the years.

First published in 2007

by

Bennett, Coleman & Co. Ltd.

7, Bahadur Shah Zafar Marg

New Delhi-110 002

All rights reserved

No part of this work may be reproduced or used in any form or by any means (graphic, electronic, mechanical, photocopying, recording, taping, web distribution, information storage and retrieval systems or otherwise) without prior written permission of the publisher.

ISBN :- 978-81-89906-02-3

For sale in India only

Compiled by	: Narayani Ganesh
Editorial Team	: Kalpana Joshi, Thoisana Singh
Cover Design	: Subhasish Munshi
Design	: Ashwani Madan
Printed and bound by	: Paras Offset Pvt. Ltd
Price	: Rs. 200

Preface

CAN the spiritual, the transcendent, have a place in something that of necessity has to be so topical and time bound a forum as a newspaper? We, in *The Times of India,* believe that the answer is an emphatic "yes". For, we believe that the legitimate realm of the spiritual is not in sequestered monasteries or in the lofty towers of philosophical thought alone. It is very much an integral part of our lives, of our thoughts and actions, and can motivate in us right personal, social and political impulses. We cannot avoid or escape these daily Kurukshetras of the mind and the soul. All we can hope to do, as Arjuna did with the help of Krishna, is to learn to realise that while we must act in the face of moral and ethical ambiguities we can try and do so without the material attachments alone determining our actions. This is where *The Speaking Tree* provides a grove of contemplative tranquillity, a sanctuary of the spirit where we can find strength to face anew the conflicts and the confrontations that are part of our human predicament. While occasionally eminent seers have contributed to *The Speaking Tree* column, most often, it is the so-called common citizen who is the author of these pieces — which is as it should be. For the world of the spirit is not out there or invested in some teacher or guru; it is our common heritage, ours to claim and ours to nurture. Welcome to its shade.

Indu Jain

New Delhi
August 2007

Contents

Celebrations
1. Celebrating Christmas Around the World 11
2. Say it With Flowers: Phoolwalon-ki-Sair 13
3. Celebrating Revelation of the Holy Qur'an 15
4. Festive Dussehra Is Full of Spiritual Nuances 17
5. Learn as You Celebrate the Festive Season 19
6. The Sacred Feminine: Durga Brings Joy 21
7. Adoration of the Divine Mother During Navratri 23
8. Celebrate the Spirit of Krishna Consciousness 25
9. Climb to Heaven in the Garden of Eden 27
10. Why We Celebrate the Birthday of Rama 29
11. Celebrating Life: Feast of Passover 31

One And Many
12. So Many Ramayanas, So Many Ramas 33
13. Dharma & Religion: Many Paths to One 35
14. Many Paths to the Summit That Offers But One View ...37
15. Vedanta As the Source of Not One But Many Truths 39
16. One Question, Many Answers To the Mystery of Life ...41
17. Existence That Operates Behind Individuality 43
18. Multidimensional Spiritual Reality 45
19. Enjoy Differences For Variety Spices Life 47
20. Individuals as Subsets of a Higher Set 49

Role Models
21. Why You Shouldn't Look For Superhumans in Avatars ...51
22. Swami Vivekananda: The Manager Monk 53
23. An American's Love For Durga 55
24. A Tale of Two Yogis: Yogananda & Babaji 57
25. Divine Import of Krishna Leela 59
26. A Temple For the Goddess of Animal 61
27. Prince of Ayodhya, Prophet of Peace 63
28. Situation Vacant: Saviour Wanted 65
29. A Glowing Tribute To the Tenth Guru 67
30. A Kondh's Love For Life and Dharani 69
31. When Chaplin Got Convinced of Gandhi's Philosophy 71

Music Divine
32. Music-Bhakti Combination Is Vital For Moksha 73
33. Experience the Mystic Resonance of Voice 75
34. Make Music in Tempest and in Quietude 77
35. Salve For the Soul in Sound of Music 79
36. Sangeet Marga: Path to Moksha 81
37. Singing For the Grace of God 83
38. Shabad-Kirtan: The Highway of Bliss 85

39.	Music Dissolves All Divisions	87
40.	Spirituality, the Soul of Our Music	89
41.	Moving Monsoon Ragas Help Unite Self With Nature	91

Happiness And Bliss

42.	Sweeping Wisdom From a Youth in Haridwar	93
43.	Mathematical Equation For Eternal Happiness	95
44.	Why Krishna Watched As Gopis Lifted Water	97
45.	Why Children Smile a Lot and Adults Are Grouchy	99
46.	Achieve Eternal Premananda by Becoming a Gopi	101
47.	The Happiness Factor in Natural Evolution	103
48.	Transform Your Mind To Be Content and Happy	105
49.	Love 24X7 Takes You To the State of Everlasting Joy	107
50.	Knowledge, Not Experience, Is Path To Anubhava	109
51.	Logical Deduction For Happiness In Life	111
52.	To Be Happy, Be Free From Any Image of Self	113
53.	Guru Retails Bliss, Not Happiness	115
54.	The Parable of the Blissful Madman	117

Art Of Giving

55.	The Kindly Stranger To Your Rescue	119
56.	Right Words Can Heal Your Heart	121
57.	Metta Bhavna For Good Health	123
58.	Look a Gift Horse in the Mouth	125
59.	Altruism, Essence of All Knowledge	127
60.	Getting Connected With Compassion	129
61.	Pass Around a Precious Gift This Season	131
62.	Steer Your Mind To Selfless Service	133
63.	The Act of Giving Spontaneously	135

Thanksgiving

64.	Significance of Giving Heartfelt Thanks	137
65.	Give Thanks: It's Part of Spiritual Evolvement	139
66.	Day of Forgiveness and Thanksgiving	141
67.	Accept Good and Bad With Gratitude	143
68.	Shukriya, Dhanyavaad, Thank You Very Much	145
69.	Tribute to Parents Who Give Us Their All	147

Science And Faith

70.	Belief In Brahmn Is No Longer Blind Faith	149
71.	Darwin As Avatar of Elective Consciousness	151
72.	There's Order in Realms of Physics and Metaphysics	153
73.	Two and Two Could Make More Than Four	155
74.	Human Behaviour Through the Prism of Science	157
75.	There's More to Gut Feeling Than We Thought	159
76.	Faith Stranger Than Dan Brown Fiction	161
77.	The Source Is Still With Us, Say Science and Religion	163
78.	Really Speaking, There Are No Scientists Or Seers	165
79.	A Physicist's Faith In Science & God	167
80.	Mapping the Physical and Mental Universes	169

Law Of Karma

81. Prevent the Influx of Karma Particles 171
82. Karma and Predestination Are Not Contradictory 173
83. Remove Blockages and Transform Your Life 175
84. Your Karma Empowers You 177
85. It's Karma At Work, Don't Blame God 179
86. Karma and the Fine Art of Remapping Our Memories ...181
87. Three Aspects of Karma Distinguish One's Actions 183
88. Decipher the Colour Code of Your Karma 185
89. Dispassionate View of the Law of Karma 187

Healing Touch

90. Oneness and Wellness the Energetic Way 189
91. Detoxify Yourself During Festival of Paryushana 191
92. Fasting Or Feasting, the Choice Is Yours 193
93. Balance the Spiritual and the Material 195
94. Relax to Overcome the Burnout Phenomenon 197
95. Don't Give in to Stress, Just Learn to Manage it 199
96. Mandala of Healing Ragas Part of Cosmic Energy 201
97. Preoccupation With Hurt Halts Healing Process 203
98. Surya the Sun God, Eternal Healer 205
99. T'ai Chi Is Difference Between Life and Death 207

Celebrating Christmas Around the World

By Marguerite Theophil

IN a foreign country over Christmas, with real snow on the ground, I desperately missed the family singing of carols, I even missed the bottle-brush type "fir" trees of my Mumbai childhood, over which we carefully thinned and fluffed out strips of cotton wool "snow"— that drifted all over the room once we turned on the fan.

Over instant pot-noodles, piles of buttered toast, and bottles of cheap wine, those of us with nowhere to go had wonderful conversations about different Christmas customs in our home-countries.

Maarit from Finland "gave" us the tradition of Advent candles. There are three Advent Sundays before Christmas. On the first Sunday in Advent, one candle is lit and placed in a special candlestick that holds four. The next Sunday, two are lit, and so on till the fourth Sunday, all are brightly shining. In some homes, the candles are placed before a window where they can be seen from the outside.

On Christmas Eve, Avi informed us, his Iraqi Christian family gathered together as one of the children read about the birth of Jesus and others held up lighted candles. After the reading, a bonfire of thorn bushes was lit. When the fire died down, each person jumped over the ashes three times, making special wishes for the coming year.

On Christmas day, a larger bonfire was lit in the churchyard, where the bishop, carrying a life-size figure of Baby Jesus, led the service. Afterwards, he blessed one person with a touch. That person touched the person next to him and the touch was passed around until all present felt the "touch of peace".

Rosa taught us about the "Posadas" in Mexico, enactments of looking for lodging for Los Peregrinos or The Pilgrims, actually Mary and Joseph, going to Bethlehem for the Census, according to the Scriptures. The Peregrinos will ask for lodging in three different houses, and get refused at the first two—showing how the Holy Family, with a heavily pregnant Mary, was told: "There's no room at the inn..." Only the third house will allow them in. That will be the house that is supposed to have the Posada for that evening. Once the "innkeepers" let them in, the group of guests comes into the home and kneels around the Nativity scene to pray the Rosary.

Katya told us that in Ukraine, two days before Christmas hay was spread on the floor of their living room as a reminder that

Christ was born not in a warm home, but in a humble manger. Her grandmother went so far as to turn off most of the heating in that room, too! A small table with a beautifully embroidered cloth holds a special bread, kolach, that has a lit candle stuck into it, to remind us that Christ is the "Bread of Life", and the "Light of the World".

To remember the star of Bethlehem, Beata informed us that in Poland the Christmas meal does not begin until the first star appears in the sky. The feast is made up of 12 courses, one for each apostle. An extra place is always set at the table for a stranger—the Holy Spirit—to share the meal.

Many of these traditions are now absorbed as part of my personalised rituals of this holy season, and I have heard from several friends of how they too have "borrowed" and woven together more meaningful celebrations for themselves.

May your Christmas be richly blessed with meaningfulness.

Say it With Flowers: Phoolwalon-ki-Sair

By Pranav Khullar

HE nip in the evening autumn air in Delhi is a sign that it's now time to celebrate the interfaith bonding festival of flower-sellers, known as Phoolwalon-ki-Sair. The annual event celebrates the rich cultural mosaic that binds together in an intricate pattern, Hindus and Muslims in India. The unique bondage that expresses itself colourfully during the flower-sellers' festival has a far deeper and eclectic origin than one might imagine. Popular among all "from artisans to aristocrats"—as Maheshwar Dayal put it—the festival is a happy occasion for communities to bond and revivify the spirit of the common man, as each participant joins in the procession to offer flowers and pankhas or fans at the Dargah of Qutubuddin Bakhtiar Kaki and the ancient temple of Jogmaya/Yogmaya at Mehrauli, Delhi.

Akbar Shah II's queen had vowed to offer a chadar and flower pankha at the Dargah of Hazrat Qutubuddin Bakhtiar Kaki and a pankha at the Yogmaya mandir, if her wish for the safe return of her son Mirza Jehangir—from his exile at Allahabad—was fulfilled. Not only did the wish come true, but the incident initiated this unique festival of floral offerings at the Dargah and the temple every year, that got revived through the efforts of Yogeshwar Dayal with the encouragement of Jawaharlal Nehru.

Common roots are reflected in the mystical dimensions of both faiths and it is interesting that the twin focus of the offerings on this occasion are both deeply mystical places. The Dargah is that of one of the most well-known mystics of the Chisti Silsilah and the direct successor of Khwaja Moinuddin Chisti, Qutubuddin Bakhtiar Kaki, who stood at the crossroads of the Sufi-Yogic syncretism, as it were. His chosen successor was Baba Farid, one of the earliest to use the common vernacular to express this mystical vision. The call of the Sufi is the mystical emotional outpouring of the heart which reaches out to the Self by encompassing all selves in its compassion.

The other place of offering, the ancient temple of Yogmaya/Jogmaya, is believed to date back to the Mahabharata, and is dedicated to Jogmaya, the reincarnation of the Goddess Mother, the infant sister of Krishna who escapes from the hands of Kansa in Mathura, and predicts his doom at the hands of the eighth-born of Devaki in an Akashvani before disappearing into the ether. Since the site is traditionally believed to be spiritually charged, the Mehrauli-temple complex has been home and witness to the sadhana of many a yogi and faqir. The call of the yogi is the austere disciplining of the mind which reaches out to the Self by silencing all thought-processes that arise.

Robert Frost wrote: "Two roads diverging in the woods... I took the one less travelled, And that has made all the difference..." The festival of flowers and floral tributes, spreading the message of spiritual brotherhood through the fragrance of its offerings, is perhaps very like that road less travelled, distinct from the highway of life, but the one which we all go back to at some point to rest awhile from the panic and paranoia of everyday life.

Celebrating Revelation of the Holy Qur'an

By Maulana Wahiduddin Khan

oza or abstinence is observed in the month of Ramadan, ninth in the Hijri calendar. It is an exercise aimed at controlling desires, and so is essentially the art of desire management. Ramadan is the month of patience. God has given us free will to test if we are able to use freedom properly.

A believer is like a tethered horse that moves only as far as its rope allows it to. One needs to tie oneself willingly with the rope of God's laws. Therefore, one who fasts imposes self-discipline and surrenders to the will of God.

The Qur'an makes special mention of its revelation in the month of Ramadan. There is a close link between Ramadan and the Qur'an. Now, if we ponder upon the relationship between the two, we find that while roza teaches us self-discipline, the Qur'an guides us on a spiritual path that enables us to manage our lives rightly.

Ramadan is the annual reminder of this blessing. The celebration of the revelation of the Qur'an is observed through abstinence and being thankful to the Almighty. Fasting in this month is acknowledgement of Divine blessings. This is a special month when the Qur'an is read and understood. The Qur'an also clearly states that when you keep a fast, you are not to do or say foul things and if someone provokes you, you are just to say: "I have kept a fast." In this way, roza makes you a unilateral subscriber to a code of ethics.

A Hadith says that two people who undertook the fast began to backbite. Prophet Muhammad said that these people had kept the fast legitimately, by abstaining from food and water, but they broke it with an illegitimate action, by engaging in "ghibat" or backbiting. Prophet Muhammad said that one who keeps roza but does not stop lying or practising wrong ways, derives no benefit. Thus, to practise abstention during Ramadan includes abstaining from wrong practices.

Fasting is a special deed. It makes the practitioner kind-hearted, and helps to awaken his inner consciousness. He is then able to feel and experience what God desires.

In rozas, after consuming food at dawn (sehri) one has not to partake of any food or water for the rest of the day till the roza is broken at dusk (iftaar). During roza, often you are able to feel the presence of God. You tend to count your blessings, and offer thanksgiving for all that has made life possible. The temporary deprivation of food and water makes you realise the importance of being blessed with divine Grace.

Roza also reminds us that all that one has is because of the Supreme, that what has been given could one day be taken away. We're here for a test. It breaks down your arrogance and stubbornness. Rozas make you realise the reality of life, that we could be helpless if not for God's Grace. In this context, it is heartfelt prayer that uplifts and affirms. Prayers help us connect with higher consciousness and so with the Supreme.

Ramadan is a month of spiritual activism when devotees try to awaken their innate spirituality. It is a scheme to improve human beings. Roza is for personality and intellectual development. This is done by desire management, experiencing helplessness and connecting to God with true prayers. This should become the way of life for the whole year. This makes observing rozas the most rewardable act—and not the mere act of abstaining from food and water.

Festive Dussehra Is Full of Spiritual Nuances

By B K Rohan

AN intriguing and interesting collection of mythological legends and diverse regional folklore is embroidered around the enormously popular festival of Dussehra or Vijayadashami that commemorates the triumph of righteousness over demonic viciousness.

In Brahmakumari philosophy, the soul, in originality, was a sparkling star-like point of conscient energy, an embodiment of pristine peace, purity and bliss, spiritually charged and residing in the golden-red light incorporeal world or the sixth element, referred to as Shantidham or Muktidham, a world beyond the gross world of five elements. When the empowered soul first descended on earth to play its predestined role, its sublime purity naturally manifested itself through the mortal body or costume it wore, in the form of divine virtues like love, happiness and joy.

Gradually, as it got entwined in the cycle of birth and death, it started falsely identifying itself with its perishable body and forgot its eternal soul-identity. It started getting attracted to the senses and sense objects that it encountered on its journey. The golden deer which allured Sita in the Ramayana is a symbolic representation of these attractions. The internal stage of soul-consciousness is indicated by the Lakshman Rekha which Sita transgressed. This led to her getting abducted by Ravana and getting distanced from Rama. The episode of abduction of Sita by Ravana refers to the abduction of the soul by the diabolical forces of evil or the five vices—lust, anger, greed, attachment and ego. Ravana, also called Dashanan, had 10 heads. These 10 heads undeniably have a symbolical, metaphorical and deep spiritual significance.

Lust, anger and greed mislead and confuse; they distract and even destroy. The soul under the influence of body-consciousness or Ravana—which literally means "one who makes you weep"—divorced itself from Rama, as a result of which it unlocked the gates of hell for itself and experienced agony and pain. Today, every soul or Sita entrapped in the fetters of vices—which are the root of all emotional sufferings, tensions and sorrows—cries out to Rama for liberation.

Rama is just one of the attributive names of the Incorporeal Supreme Father of all souls. He is eternally bodiless and is an inhabitant of Shantidham, free from the cycle of birth and rebirth and constantly peaceful, pure, blissful and full of love.

The allegory relates to the advent of the Supreme soul at the end of Kaliyuga in the corporeal world to emancipate all Sitas from adversity and hardship. According to His sacred promise in the Gita, the Supreme Being incarnates at such a pivotal juncture when souls have become slaves of satanic impulses and carnal desires. He rejuvenates and remoulds spiritually enervated souls and purifies their intellects by imparting unvitiated Gita knowledge to them. He teaches them simple Rajayoga meditation—Rajayoga can be broken up into Raja+yoga which means "king of unions"—by which souls can link their minds and intellects to him and spiritually re-empower themselves.

The word Dussehra comes from the word Dasa-Hara, Dasa meaning 10 and Hara meaning annihilated. Only when we overcome the inherent 10-headed demon of Ravana with the arrow of spiritual knowledge and incinerate his colossal effigy with the divine fire of intense meditation or yoga with the Supreme can we truly partake in and enjoy the celebration of Dussehra and experience eternal and divine bliss.

Learn as You Celebrate the Festive Season

By Sitakant Mahapatra

N my school days, Saraswati Puja was a major festival. I would gather flowers in the morning from our garden and fast the entire day. At school, we, students, decorated the idol of Saraswati with flower garlands and the pedestal with festoons and deodar leaves. The priest performed puja and we offered pushpanjali or flower offerings, chanting a hymn in chorus, following the words of the priest: "Thou who has the whiteness of kunda flowers, the moon and snow, who is seated on a white lotus, draped in white and wielding a veena in thine hands; thou whom Brahma, Achyuta, Shankara and other gods worship in divine prayers; O Saraswati, Bhagwati, we pay obeisance to you."

At the time I knew nothing of Markandeya Purana's Devi Mahatmyam, Skanda Purana or Madhusudan Stotra wherein the white goddess is described with all her attributes and powers. The Purana elaborates on the manner in which she is to be venerated. The Devi Mahatmyam speaks of her as Mahasaraswati, and describes her beauty in great detail: "She is effulgent like the moon shining at the fringe of a cloud."

When in deference to entreaties of the gods she is required to kill the formidable demons, Shumbha and Nishumbha, she transforms herself into a ferocious goddess with her eight lotus-like hands holding bells, trident, plough, conch, mace, discus, bow and arrow. In the Markandeya Purana she appears at the final phase of the vanquishing of the brood of demons who troubled the gods. This is after Mahakali, "Luminous like a blue jewel", has destroyed Madhu and Kaitabha—who had stolen the four Vedas from Brahma—and after Mahalakshmi, the coral-complexioned goddess, has decimated Mahishasura in a long battle in which the buffalo-demon assumes several illusory forms. Divine anger against the demons first rages as tamas in Mahakali, then as rajas in Mahalakshmi, and, finally, as sattva in Mahasaraswati. She has dual divinity—as the destroyer of evil and as the giver of knowledge.

She is Vagdevi, the goddess of primordial vak or the word which is the foundation of the universe, which creates us, gives us our identity and imparts meaning to our existence. The word, that is, sabda, is Parambrahmn, the Absolute. Emanating from the white goddess, the primordial vak differentiates itself into myriad words, with infinite nuances of meaning and cadences of music. It constitutes both the white light of life and the darkness of death. Sabda is composed of aksharas, which literally mean the indestructible.

Vagdevi is also the goddess of music; she has a veena in her hands. It is the music that Rabindranath Tagore speaks of as the music of the spheres. It is also the terrifying music of kettledrums, cymbals and the deafening roar which astounds Mahishasura.

The Skanda Purana says that Vagdevi wears a captivating, life-giving smile on her face, bearing ultimate wisdom in her heart. She resides in the throat and sits on the tongue of great poets and makes them vaksiddhas. A Skanda Purana prayer says: "Bless me so that when I read scriptures, when participating in learned disputations or composing poems, my wisdom is ever-expansive and let it never get inhibited." It is a prayer for total, unfettered expression. In the Madhusudan Stotra, Vagdevi is one of the Trimurti—as Svarupini, Savitri and Gayatri.

The Sacred Feminine: Durga Brings Joy

By M N Chatterjee

 DURGA Puja is the joyous celebration of the feminine principle as enunciated in the Devi Mahatmyam, without belittling the male counterpart. Shiva-Parvati and Lakshmi-Narayana are common names drawn from Hindu mythology. Shiva-Shakti represents the unity of time and eternity, the male element being the quiescent state and the feminine form the active one. Their functions are complementary.

Durga, the militant manifestation of Parvati, is the embodiment of Shakti, infinite energy created from the combined invocation and the conjoined effulgence of the gods who were driven away from heaven by rampaging demons after a lost battle. The gods gave her their powerful weaponry in a bid to strengthen Durga's hands in her fight against the ferocious fiends headed by Mahishasura, the buffalo-demon. Shiva gave her his trident, Vishnu his disc, Kubera his club, Indra his thunder and Vayu his bow and arrows. Equipped with varied weaponry and with the lion as her mount, Mahadevi Durga challenged the demons who were considered invincible. A fierce and gory battle ensued.

Once the demons were eliminated during battle, Devi faced their chief. As soon as Mahishasura saw Devi, he transformed himself from buffalo to lion. When she chopped his head off, he assumed human form. Despite his devious tactics and multiple forms, he was ultimately trapped under her foot and Durga's spear pierced his chest. But from his mouth emerged another form of the demon, half-revealed, and she cut off his head too with her sword. Peace was restored in the cosmic order. Durga came to be worshipped as Mahishasurmardini, killer of the buffalo-demon.

The 700-verse Devi Mahatmyam of the Markandeya Purana is also known as Chandi or Durgasaptsati. Its recitation every autumn is called Chandipath. Thomas Coburn hails the hymns as the crystallisation of the goddess tradition, the central concern of their articulation being the vision of ultimate reality in the universe in the persona of the goddess.

The annual re-enactment of the conflict between divine and demonic forces in the story of Mahishasurmardini during Durga Puja symbolises the eternal struggle between the forces of good and evil and the undying hope of the ultimate triumph of all that is good. The battle rages not only against external enemies confounding us with beguiling appearances but also internally between base and benign instincts in every person. The divine and human aspects coalesce in Durga's story as it marks the homecoming of the Mother Goddess for a four-day sojourn in her parental home, not unlike her human counterparts.

As Shakti, Durga has two traits: one mild represented by Bhavani, Gauri, Uma and the other, fierce, represented by Durga, Kali, Shyama, Chandi and Bhairavi. She is also Jaagaddhatri, Amba, Bhadrakali and Chamundi.

As prakriti, Durga is intimately connected with the physical world. She personifies the earth and stands for cosmic stability, sustaining all creatures. The cult of the Shakti pithas reinforces the Hindu belief that the earth is a goddess. She is also identified as maya, particularly in the Madhu-Kaitabh legend wherein she deludes the demons while helping Vishnu to subjugate them. The complex concept of maya emerges as a positive force used by the deity to overcome evil elements.

Adoration of the Divine Mother During Navratri

By Kiran Dhar

USK is falling, lamps are lit,
The autumn air is cool and still.
The bells are calling from afar
Come join in Mother's adoration hour.
   I enter slowly, my heartbeat overtakes me
   Will I see Her face to face?
   My body trembles, how shall I greet
   Dare I touch Her Holy feet?
The air is filled with incense smoke,
The priest prostrates in reverent pose.
The Mother in regal splendour stands
Enrobed in silks of red and gold.
      Glittering jewels and golden crown
      From head to feet do Her adorn.
      Hibiscus, roses, marigold
      In garlands fragrant Her form enfold.
Compassion fills Her lustrous eyes
Her coral lips are half-a-smile.
One hand is raised to grant us boons
The other dispels our deepest fears.
Her beauty is beyond compare
With radiance of a thousand moons.
      The drums are beating rhythmic time,
      The cymbals sound a resonant chime.
      The bells are ringing loud and clear,
      Conchshells sounding everywhere,
      Scent of incense fills the air,
      Devotees' voices raised in prayer,
      Glory to the Mother evermore.
Besides the Mother's shining form
A lovely maiden stands alone,
Gently turning with her hands
A silken fan of rainbow hues.
      The priest begins the evening prayer
      With sonorous chanting loud and clear.
      Then he takes the incense urn
      And all around the Mother turns.
O Holy incense, fragrant smoke
Your perfume does the Mother cloak.
Next he takes the golden lamp
Ablaze with myriad dancing flames,

Waves in circles round Her form,
Around, around and all around,
Joy in every heart abounds.
    O Holy lamp of brilliant light
    Blest you to be in Mother's sight.
    Now it is the lotus red
    Offered to the Mother's form.
    O pure and Holy lotus flower,
    May you ever at Her feet repose.
The priest now gives the final call,
"Dear brothers, sisters, come one and all,
The hour for 'anjali' draws near
Time to offer flowers and prayers."
    In answer to his solemn words
    The congregation gathers round
    With outstretched hands, to take the flowers.
    Soon each worshipper's cupped-hand bowl
    Is filled with rose petals, jasmine and marigold.
Next he intones the sacred verse,
"O mother Durga, we bow to Thee,
Grant us good fortune, health and prosperity.
Destroy our sins and remove all pain,
Forgive us for the mistakes we make.
O Mother of the World, be Thou pleased
And accept the offerings we make to Thee."
    The worship's over, silence falls,
    My heart is filled with love sublime.
    In the mirror of my heart I only see the Mother's eyes.
    O Mother Divine, from my heart I pray
    Grant to me Thy wondrous Grace.
    My only refuge is Thy lotus feet,
    Nothing else I choose to seek.

Celebrate the Spirit of Krishna Consciousness

By Chaitanya Charan Das

 HATEVER name we prefer to give the Supreme Being—Jehovah, Allah, Buddha, Shakti, Vishnu or Krishna—the concept of a Supreme Creator is that He is of extraordinary attributes and is universally attractive. The name Krishna means "the all-attractive One". "Sarva akarshati iti Krishna"—this describes the attractive nature of the Lord and so describes the absolute Truth, the supreme personality of Godhead, in full.

The Lord administers the world through the laws of material nature—gross such as the law of gravitation and subtle such as the law of karma. But when predominance of materialism over spirituality disturbs the universal order, the Lord descends "to deliver the pious, annihilate the miscreants and re-establish divine principles", says the Bhagavad Gita.

Krishna descends not just to maintain law, but to awaken love. The love that our heart longs for through relationships with various persons finds fulfilment only when it is reposed in the Supreme. When we love Krishna, our love is never interrupted, never betrayed, never let down, never disappointed.

Unfortunately, in this world of matter, all living beings are attracted not to the Lord of their heart but to matter and material enjoyment. However, matter being limited and finite, it can never fulfil the unlimited desires of our spirit; material enjoyment satiates, but never satisfies.

God comes to the material world and performs superhuman activities which reveal His supreme nature and unparalleled love for all. Krishna lifted the Govardhan Mountain in order to protect His devotees from rains. Such acts appear impossible to the sceptical mind, but an ant would similarly consider the lifting of a book by a human being as "impossible". For Krishna, possessing unlimited power, such an act is not at all difficult. Realising the infinite love of Krishna enables us to return to the kingdom of God, with Him.

On Janmashtami, Krishna entered the material world at midnight. This is significant. Midnight is the time of maximum darkness and from the moment the Lord appeared, the darkness started diminishing. Similarly, our heart is dark, being afflicted by multiple anxieties and miseries. But in the darkest hour of our lives, when we turn to Krishna, He appears in our heart, and all the darkness recedes and the light of eternal hope starts streaming in. The Lord appeared in a prison cell and then freed His parents of their shackles. This indicates that all of us who are shackled by our self-destructive desires can be freed by the Lord who appears in our heart which is obscured in darkness.

Janmashtami celebrates Krishna's presence in our hearts. Indeed, amidst all the chaos and disorder prevalent in this Kalyuga, why has the Lord not appeared as per His eternal promise in the Bhagavad Gita? The Vedic scriptures declare, "kali kale nama rupe Krishna avatar"—that in Kali Yuga, the Lord incarnates in the form of His Holy Name.

All religions recommend chanting the names of God. The Bible says: "Let the Lord always be on your lips," Islam exhorts the chanting of the 99 names of Allah. And among all the mantras—empowered sound vibrations—mentioned in Vedic scriptures, the maha-mantra: "Hare Krishna Hare Krishna Krishna Krishna Hare Hare, Hare Ram Hare Ram Ram Ram Hare Hare" is specially recommended for our age. So let us experience the love, care, protection and happiness of Janmashtami—the appearance of the Lord in our hearts—by devotedly chanting His holy names.

Climb to Heaven in the Garden of Eden

By Narayani Ganesh

VERYONE wants to go on pilgrimage to the island—whether Buddhist, Hindu, Christian or Muslim. Equally, it attracts those with no persuasion at all, for Sri Lanka's eclectic spiritual heritage makes it one of the few remaining places where animism, religious mythology, history and folklore twine to present an intriguing, yet charming kaleidoscopic view of our common spiritual evolution.

Adam's Peak rises majestically in the south of the Central Highlands, not far from the town of Ratnapura. A large footprint on a rock on top of the mountain is venerated—depending on what you like to believe—as Buddha's Sri Pada, as Nataraja's cosmic dance step, as Adam's footprint when he entered the Garden of Eden (or when he was sent here as the next best place to live in when he had to leave the biblical Garden of Eden), or as Saint Thomas the Apostle's imprint. Indigenous tribes called it Butterfly Mountain, and the Sinhalese refer to it as Samanalakanda or abode of deity Samana.

In Sri Lanka briefly, there was no time to make the pilgrimage. Dudley Fernando, our guide, quipped: "The one who climbs Adam's Peak and witnesses the glorious sunrise, catching the peak's shadow fall on the clouds, is a fortunate and wise person. But the one who returns for a second experience... is a fool!" Why, because the peak has to be reached on foot, a steep climb up the mountainside and several steps, a tiring exercise for even the fit and the determined. That's what pilgrimages are all about—the journey, rather than the destination, is what counts, the hardship and hurdles adding value to an experience that propels one to reflect and retrospect, opening doors to understanding the principle of universal oneness and harmony. It could be why the mountain is also known as the climb to heaven, or Svargarohanam.

Pan now to the Ramayana, the Hindu epic, that narrates the story of Rama, Prince of Ayodhya, and the vanquishing of Lanka's demon-king Ravana. Half-hidden in a glade of Ashoka trees, a small but ornate temple overlooks a gurgling stream in the hills of Sita Eliya, part of the tea country of Nuwara Eliya. The spot is believed to be one among the seven secluded places where Ravana confined Sita after he abducted her from her home-in-exile in the Dandakaranya forest.

There's another world out there in Kandy, only a few

kilometres away, the top pilgrimage destination for Buddhists the world over. This is where the sacred tooth of the Buddha is preserved and idolised, at the Dalada Maligawa or Tooth Temple that overlooks the pretty Kandy Lake. Devotees make offerings of lotus flower and incense stick to the accompaniment of loud drumbeats and playing of pipes.

Towards the north, at the Dambulla caves, not far from Anuradhapura with its beautiful secular and religious idols and paintings including those of the Buddha and his disciples, invocations to the Buddha are preceded by an elaborate Hindu ritual puja offered to Vishnu, the protector, conducted by a Hindu priest. Frangipani or temple flowers, lotus and lilies adorned the wooden planks placed in front of the Vishnu and Buddha idols, respectively. As we stepped out into the sun, the Hindu-Buddhist incantations became faint. The cool breeze that greeted us as we descended the hill lifted our spirits a little higher.

Why We Celebrate the Birthday of Rama

By Sri Sathya Sai Baba

THE brothers Rama, Lakshmana, Bharata and Shatrughna had total unity among themselves. Even while playing games in their childhood, each aspired for the victory of the other.

Once the four young lads were playing a game. Shortly thereafter, Bharata came to mother Kausalya, weeping. She asked him, "Bharata, why are you feeling sad? Have you lost the game?" Bharata replied, "Mother, I would have been happy if that were the case, but when I was about to lose the game, Rama managed to lose the game and made me the winner. I am upset at the defeat of my elder brother."

When Lakshmana fell unconscious in the battlefield, Rama was crestfallen. He lamented: "If I were to search in the world, I may get a mother like Kausalya and a wife like Sita but not a brother as noble as Lakshmana. What is the use of this life without Lakshmana?"

When Bharata returned from Kekaya kingdom, he came to know from Sage Vasishtha that Rama had gone into exile and would not return for 14 long years. He was disconsolate. He said: "I do not want this kingdom which has caused the exile of my brother Rama. Being the eldest son, only Rama has the right to rule over the kingdom. Hence, at this very moment I shall go to the forest, fall at the feet of Rama and plead with Him to come and reign over Ayodhya."

In order to uphold His father's word, Rama was ready to go into exile. Rama's birthday celebrations remind us of the ideals He stood for. Sage Vasishtha declared that Rama is the embodiment of Dharma. He described the Divine form of Rama as enchanting. "Rama, Your beauty is not limited to Your physical form. You are infinite love and compassion. You are the very personification of Sat-chit-ananda."

Kali yuga has become the age of kalaha or conflict. In such a scenario, the Ramayana throws light on how brothers and sisters should conduct themselves. In the Ramayana, we find demonstration of great ideals. We need to emulate those ideals. The Ramayana transcends barriers of time, space, caste and religion. In all nations, at all times and under all circumstances, unity is essential to find fulfilment in life.

There is not a single instance of internal dispute in the family of Dasaratha. Even Kaikeyi had great affection for Rama. But her mind was poisoned because of the bad company of Manthara. Hence, it is said, "Tell me your company, I shall tell you what you are." Manthara was only acting under the influence of an incident that happened in her previous birth.

The Ramayana is compared to the Vedas. It teaches the pravritti and nivritti aspects of life. Pravritti is the swabhava (nature) of prakriti. Nivritti is the swarupa (form) of the atma. Nivritti broadens our outlook, whereas pravritti does the opposite. Hence, we should base all our activities on nivritti.

The Ramayana teaches the principles of Dharma and the path of duty to every individual. Though ages and aeons have passed by, the Ramayana remains ever fresh, guiding humanity on the path of truth and righteousness. Even today we think of the characters of Ramayana with respect and reverence. The Ramayana should be the subject of our parayana (worship). Install the principle of Rama in your heart and experience bliss.

Celebrating Life: Feast of Passover

By Ezekiel Isaac Malekar

ESACH is one of the most significant Jewish festivals. Passover is being celebrated for eight days. Pesach commemorates Israel's liberation from Egyptian bondage, when a free people awakened to the determination to serve none but the One God. The festival is, therefore, called Zeman Cheruthenu, the season of our liberty.

As the emancipated slaves went out of Egypt in great haste, they could carry only unleavened dough with them. Therefore, during the entire Pesach week, unleavened bread known as matza is eaten. That's why Pesach is also known as Hag Hamatzoth, the feast of unleavened bread.

A famine ravished Canaan when Jacob and his family sought refuge on the east bank of the Nile. His descendants grew into a large nation; most of them lived in the Goshen region of Egypt. As time passed, their situation steadily deteriorated and ultimately they became mere slaves of the pharaohs. They suffered for 210 years. At last Moses and Aharon were sent to the royal court with the Divine message: "Shallah eth ammi veyavduni"—Let My people go, that they may serve Me. The pharaoh refused to pay heed and brought upon himself and his people the consequent onslaught of the 10 plagues. Later, when the Hebrew slaves were freed, they went out of Egypt.

Pesach is coined from the Hebrew verb "passah" meaning "to pass over". It is the sacrifice of the Lord's pass over, for that He passed over the houses of the children of Israel in Egypt, when He smote the Egyptians and delivered our houses. The Israelites had smeared the blood of the Paschal lamb on their doorposts at God's specific command and they were spared by the Angel of Death.

Pesach is initiated by a service in the synagogue, followed by the home Seder that literally means Order, a special meal with accompanying ritual commemorative of the exodus from Egypt. During the Seder, the tale of Passover is read. The ceremonial meal begins with chanting of the sanctification prayer. After washing hands, the participants take the leaf of parsley or watercress which symbolise growth and spring, dip it in salt water, recite the blessing and eat it. The salt water is a reminder of tears shed by enslaved Goshen Jews. On the Seder plate, the following too are seen: the roasted shank bone of a lamb, symbolising Paschal lamb; a roasted egg, symbolising the holiday sacrifice; horse radish, symbolising the bitterness of slavery and a mixture of apples, raisins, cinnamon and wine that symbolise the clay of Egypt with which the Hebrew slaves were forced to make bricks.

Usually, the youngest in the family recites the four questions of the Haggadah including why Seder is observed. Four cups of wine, standing for four distinct promises made to the Israelites, are drunk during the feast. There is a special cup filled with wine, called Kos shel Eliyahu, the cup of the Prophet Elijah who, according to Jewish legend, visits every Seder, and who, at the end of days, will bring the tidings of the Messianic age. To reaffirm the faith in his coming, the main door of the house is kept open during the feast to admit him. Traditional Hebrew songs are sung by all in unison.

The Seder has survived in the Jewish home through every exigency of history and persists as an emblem and promise of freedom. It ever was, and still is, the high spot of religious home ceremonies.

So Many Ramayanas, So Many Ramas

By Amrith Lal

ALAYALAM short story writer V P Sivakumar once said that life teaches every individual to read the Ramayana. It took me a long while to understand what he meant. Now I wonder, does every individual write his own Ramayana?

Valmiki's Ramkatha lives off the limits of space and time. The story was there before the sage, and after him. The itihasa kavya continues to live in many forms, many tongues; each actually narrating a new story.

How many Ramayanas are there? A K Ramanujan once attempted to answer the question. He first counted 300, added another 100, only to be told by a Kannada writer that there are over 1,000 of them in his language alone. Ramanujan summed up the count by recounting a Hindi folk tale:

"*Once, Rama lost his ring. Hanuman was told to look for it. He travelled the worlds in search of the lost ring. At last, he reached the netherworld, where he was taken to the King of the Spirits who showed him a platter of rings. There were thousands of them, all belonging to Rama. 'Take your pick,' Hanuman was told. When he pleaded for help since all of them looked the same, the king said: 'There have been as many Ramas as there are rings on this platter. When you return to earth, you will not find Rama. This incarnation of Rama is now over. Whenever an incarnation of Rama is about to be over, his ring falls down. I collect them and keep them'.*"

For each Rama, there is a Ramayana. Since there are many Ramas, there are many Ramayanas; each reflecting the age in which it is narrated. In the centuries when the Bhakti movement flourished across India, Valmiki's maryada purusha made way for the divine philosopher-king of Kamban and Ezhuthachhan. For Kabir and Thyagaraja, who followed them, Rama was an abstract ideal. So was it for Gandhi who weaved in an ethical concept of Ramrajya into his narrative of a free India.

Is the Ramayana, then, a mere story or an allegory on the struggle between good and evil? Or is it a chunk of history elaborated as a narrative of a nation? Ramayana is all these, and perhaps more. It is history, a story, an allegory; more than anything it is a tradition of narratives. Every individual continues to author it throughout his life to make it his own tale.

As a child, the Ramayana is a bedtime story: "Once upon a

time in a faraway land called Ayodhya, there was a king called Dasharatha..." Here Rama is the obedient son, the aspiration of every father and mother. In adulthood, you are initiated into Rama, the sthithapragnya, who would explain to Lakshmana the ways of the world as "paandhar peruvazhiyambalam thannile/ thantarai koodi viyogum varumbole"—"tired people arriving in rest houses, only to depart soon". The text grows on you with time. Life, indeed, teaches you to read it. And, in many ways.

The narrative reaches a dead end the minute it is historicised. Constrained to the co-ordinates of space and time, it ceases to be a story, an idea. The itihasa as a narrative of nation drops out of the realm of imagination. The Rama of Kalidasa's Raghuvamsa is a marching hero; the marauding empire builder of orthodoxy sweeping the plains of Aryavarta. In the 20th century, he was bundled into a rath to take on the imagined Other of the "defeated Hindu". History repeats itself as farce, shorn of poetry. The yoke of history is a burden to the story. It demeans the soul of the narrative. Return Rama to the story. Let it be, as the Yoga Vasishta says, "the raft with which men will cross the ocean of samsara". As Kabir put it: "Ram's pass is a high one/ Kabir keeps climbing..."

Dharma & Religion: Many Paths to One

By M V Mehta

A four-line verse of wisdom in Sanskrit—Subhashit—pronounces the commonness among animals and men of certain primal appetites and urges and proclaims the supremacy of Dharma in man's actions and life, without which he would be no different from animals. Here, Dharma is to be understood as encompassing man's entire life, including all his thoughts and deeds, and is not to be confused with any religion.

Dharma has been defined in dictionaries as the essential quality or character of everything severally or together, such as of the cosmos or one's nature and conformity with cosmic law, rita, or largely understood religious law, custom, duty or one's quality or inalienable character. This definition, understood in its widest implication, is expected to be observed in interpreting a man's internal thought process and external actions which, if found to be in exact congruence, can be seen as being dharmic and which elevates human beings above all other animate beings.

The meaning of Dharma is threaded through every atom of the created cosmos, anusyut, and has been already illuminated in our vast shruti and smriti literature and the insightful commentaries on them by great savants, seers, and sages like Adi Shankaracharya. A very brief, formulaic pointer—Dharanat Dharma, that upholds Dharma—can be kept as reference. In any field of life, on any occasion, in whatever circumstances, the carrying out of one's natural function and upholding one's responsibility in balanced action, always remembering one's humanity, ensuring one's spiritual welfare, and avoiding disintegration in mundane pursuits (shreya and preya) is Dharma.

The head of the dharmic man has to remain above the ocean of sansara which constantly tries to sink him in the murky waters of material and sensuous pleasures and worldly wealth by negative actions. When you observe the precepts of the religion of your choice, you are sure to see life conforming to the description of Dharma briefly outlined above. Of course, observances and rituals vary from one religion to another. Also, there are separate beliefs concerning the cause, nature and purpose of the universe when seen as the creation of a superhuman being or beings and involving devotional and ritual practices under a moral code for followers. This is the visible aspect of religion, but the internal religious experience relates to the being seen as the Creator-God, the goal of all devotees. God is the only entity who is omniscient, omnipresent, and omnipotent. He has no name and form, is beyond the reach of mind and language, and can be experienced as the light in the devotee's heart. Naming of this being differently by different religions, and fanatical adherence to the names by followers, tend to spark conflict. Ironically, religions accept God to be One without a second.

Forgetting the divisions, it is essential to accept all religions as paths to the same One God. Paths are innumerable. Indian spiritual, philosophical, and scriptural literature and different group practices comprise several and distinguishable approaches which are characterised as matas (bodies of beliefs) also included in different paths to God. God is unconcerned with the paths. He cares only for devotees approaching Him along any of them. All names, being man-given, are imperfect and inappropriate, but He cares not for names. He responds to the soul cry of the devotee, which is known as prayer, and waits with open arms to receive him. Prayer is man's most potent tool for salvation. He who knows and accepts this is a true follower of religion, irrespective of the name by which it is.

Many Paths to the Summit That Offers But One View

By Sensei Sandeep Desai

IKE eating, sleeping and brushing your teeth, T'ai Chi or yoga should become part of your daily regimen. At first, it might seem difficult to establish the habit. But a few months later, the benefits become so obvious that it's hard to break away from regular practice.

During the week, people tend to leap out of bed the moment the alarm rings, jump into the shower, and rush off to work—and all this while, their bodies are still technically "asleep". This kind of routine places tremendous strain on heart and brain. Thirty minutes of early morning T'ai Chi not only prevents such self-inflicted damage to the body, but also helps you to tackle the rest of the day in better ways.

There are a number of reasons never to miss a day of T'ai Chi practice. One reason is that a certain continuity is necessary for progress. If a day is missed, there is a strong possibility that the mind will lose the thread of both what has been learned in class and what has been worked on. When an insight or breakthrough is imminent, it is important that the vehicle for its actualisation be available. Missing a day makes the next day harder and less efficient. When you are active, a certain momentum begins to build up. When you are inactive, a corresponding inertia prevails and becomes increasingly difficult to overcome.

Missing a day's practice could lead to another day being missed and so on. Chinese Grandmaster Zhu Tian Cai says, "Ten minutes of T'ai Chi is better than 10 minutes more of sleep." At the end of the day when I think I am too tired to do the form, I remember his words. After 10 minutes of practice, I am frequently so energised that I end up practising much more than 10 minutes. When I go to bed, my sleep is much deeper and better than if I had not practised. The next day I experience an increased efficiency. Moreover, daily practice over a period of time results in a lowering of the need for sleep by much more than the time spent practising.

As you practise, you will discover new details, experience new body feelings, and become more integrated. Your mind will become calm, clear and focused inward. Your movements will take on a softer, smoother, more effortless quality, and you will begin to develop a T'ai Chi body. One day you will be surprised by your skill.

One of the most important dividends gained from the study of

T'ai Chi is an approach to learning. An approach to learning is much more valuable than any subject matter because it can be applied to any subject matter. T'ai Chi is not the only way to the top of the mountain. T'ai Chi is not better than Yoga. For some, it is better.

For others, it may not be. Ranking exercise programmes or belief systems is not necessary because everybody is different and what is an A+ to one person may be a D- to another. Different things appeal to different people and effect people differently. If it works for you, it just works. And that's great. For there are many paths to the top of the mountain, but when you get there, the view is the same.

Vedanta As the Source of Not One But Many Truths

By Malay Mishra

N Kathopanishad, Nachiketa, the young seeker of truth, dared to question Yama, the Lord of Death. He asks Yama what happens to human beings once the body dies. No amount of persuasion would deter Nachiketa from his jijnasa and Yama has to yield, for he realises that Nachiketa is sincere in his desire to know the truth in his lifetime.

Yama's reply to Nachiketa is part of Yajurveda, where the Upanishads constitute the Jnana Kanda portion at the end, also referred to as Vedanta. Upanishad literally means "teaching bestowed while sitting near". It also means "destroying ignorance completely". In Brihadaranyaka, Sage Yajnavalkya's conversations with wife Maitreyi and with Vachaknavi Gargi, reveal true knowledge that becomes clear once layers of ego, ignorance, conceit and arrogance are systematically overcome.

Through questioning the fundamentals of human existence, philosophers arrived at truths and by speculating on physical facts, Vedic thinkers arrived at a unitary conception of the universe. Theirs was a cosmological monism through the concepts of avyakta, indeterminate nature, neti, ontological negation and prana, cosmic energy. The culmination of their discovery was the unification of all experience in the atman or Brahmn.

The common strand in Upanishadic thought is love of truth and its fearless quest epitomising the courage of human inquiry in delving deep into the mysteries of life. Romain Rolland observed: "True Vedantic spirit does not start out with a system of preconceived ideas. It possesses absolute liberty and unrivalled courage among religions with regard to the facts to be observed. Never having been hampered by the priestly order, each man has been entirely free to search wherever he pleased for the spiritual explanation of the spectacle of the universe."

Chandogya Upanishad talks about the fearless cart driver, Raikwa, who chastises the mighty king for carting material riches to him to tempt him to pass on his spiritual knowledge. "Have neither pride nor vanity, O King, in the charities you dispense. Give not something as yours but as something given to you by the Spirit for giving to others. He who sees this truth becomes a seer because for him nothing is wanting anymore," says Raikwa.

The path of bhakti to a personal God, the path of karma or

detached action, the path of jnana or the fire of knowledge and the synthesis of all paths in a comprehensive spirituality as expounded in Bhagavad Gita, are all derived from the Upanishads. Kathopanishad's telling words: "Uthistata, jagrata, prapya varan nibodhata"—Arise! Awake! and stop not till the goal is reached—were carried by Swami Vivekananda to the farthest corners of the world and, in so doing, he realised the Upanishadic ideal of the rivers of knowledge flowing from all sides into the Ocean of Jnana that resides within the self. "Tat Tvam Asi", proclaims Ishopanishad, the mahavakya, denoting the spiritual unfolding of the human being at its highest.

Is the Self an originator or experiencer? In the final instance, it is the Brahmn which wills all and, thus, weaves an elaborate world of Maya in which we live. The Mundaka says that the Self is established in the luminous city of Brahmn which is the heart of man.

One Question, Many Answers To the Mystery of Life

By Pranav Khullar

 basic question—whether there is a meaning and purpose to our existence—arises in, and perhaps bothers, the mind of every individual, whether the doubt is articulated or not, as he gets through his everyday life. Scholars and philosophers, since long, have mulled over questions regarding our existence.

Is our existence a random event in evolution or is there a greater principle in life with meaning and purpose? This inquiry served as catalyst for the history of ideas, the philosophical and scientific quests, a trigger for some of the greatest spiritual odysseys. "...These indestructible questions... cannot be kept simmering on a back burner for long. They will thunder loudly in the emptiness within you, in moments of personal crisis or when you've lost your social moorings", wrote T Z Lavine.

Is there an all-encompassing Over-mind or Absolute Spirit in which all concepts are unified? Is reality a complex totality of rational concepts? Hegel's dialectical method of reasoning allowed him to view the world from a teleological perspective. On the other hand, is an understanding of the structures of "consciousness", as Husserlian phenomenology would have it, enough to gain insights into the mystery of the mind of man? Is there no meaning at all, as Sartre pointed out? Are we condemned to be free to live out our lives? The Upanishads say, "neti, neti"—not this, not this—is that something beyond our intellectual grasp; is it only what lies in the stillness beyond the working of the mind, the Sat-chit-ananda or Existence-consciousness-bliss of Vedantic thought? Swami Sivananda pointed out that real yoga is to discipline the vikshepa or tossing of the mind which will enable one to experience the stillness beyond through meditation. This existence could be maya or illusion, as Sankara's Advaita and Nagarjuna's Shunyavada would have us believe; a vivarata, an unreal appearance only. Or, could there be a meaning to this phenomenal world?

Suffering, whether personal or otherwise, is at times a catalyst to go beyond surface realities and attempt to understand the purpose of life. Viktor Frankl, out of his personal experiences as a Holocaust survivor, wrote: "ultimately, man should not ask what the meaning of his life is, but rather, must recognise that it is he who is asked... each man is questioned by life; to life he can only respond by being responsible". He goes on to say that one can try and discover a meaning in life by doing a deed, experiencing a value or by suffering. For, hasn't it been said that the road less travelled is the spiritual path, right next to the regular highway of life? By the very nature of its questioning and search, life is a difficult and arduous path. Prince Siddhartha took off on this path to search for meaning and purpose, which he found in the Buddha state of mind.

There are no universal answers, but each time the question is asked, it throws up a different answer, unique to each individual. It is this enquiry, "Athato Brahmn Jignasa"—now, therefore, the enquiry into Brahmn—from the first sutra of the Brahmn sutras, which is essential to be asked, for the search to start for a deeper and more enduring value. The philosophic quest is a call to that enquiry, and the answers may be as varied as nature itself.

Existence That Operates Behind Individuality

By Acharya Mahaprajna

N individual has two aspects: his individuality and the essential existence. Existence means to be aware of being alive. Individuality means to be something. When we mark name and form, we observe individuality. When we observe the degree of awareness, we see the existence that operates behind the individuality.

As an individual, Mahavira is the originator of an order, the spokesman of the dharma of order and the initiator of a system. So far as his existence is concerned, he simply is. To be existent is his essence. Essentially, he is neither a preceptor nor a follower, neither a spokesman of a dharma nor a listener, neither a dualist nor a non-dualist.

Dual and non-dual, interpretation and acceptance, theological law-giving and submission to it are all branches of individuality. Through his life, Mahavira moves from individuality to existence.

Seeing these maxims, a non-dualist will say that Mahavira was a non-dualist. A student of Jainism will be confused why Mahavira, being a dualist, adopted the terminology of a non-dualist. Mahavira is away from both. He is a votary of existence. The non-dual and the dual, both originate from existence. Hence, a votary of existence sometimes borrows the idiom of non-dualism and sometimes that of dualism.

"To be something" implies discrimination. In it, the latencies of violence are present, still. None would wish injury or violence to oneself. If no self is different from me, how would I kill anybody? On the plane of existence, it is a "unititive" experience. This is non-violence. The self is violence and the self is non-violence. The concept of difference and discrimination between the self and self is violence and the concept of identity between the self and self is non-violence. In "to be" (alone) the question of identity and difference does not arise. On this plane, only "to be" is true.

On the plane of individuality, Mahavira's logic is different. He says: "Kill no creature." He would say: "As you shun pain, so do other creatures." In their common aversion to pain, the killer and the killed have the same identity. Observing this common characteristic would quench all urge to violence.

Mahavira's orientation was towards existence, hence, individual distinctions never barred his progress. A votary of existence does not regard an individual as an individual but as truth, as a radiance of conscious self. His piercing eye goes beyond individuality to where existence is. In that transcendental context, questions of who and whose follower have no relevance. Such narrow considerations arise only in the petty context of individuality.

Truth is the norm in the domain of existence and pragmatism in that of individuality. Mahavira was a votary of existence but he was aware of the expectations of an individual. To advance an individual towards pure existence, his individuality was also to be made instrumental. Mahavira said, "Monks! Before discussing religion with an individual, keep in mind who he is and whose votary he is."

Triumph and defeat bear significance for an individualist. A votary of existence is indifferent to both.

Multidimensional Spiritual Reality

By S H Venkatramani

TRUE spirituality is beyond thought—it is transcendent and, therefore, incomprehensible. How can we describe something that's beyond comprehension?

Hindu philosophy stresses the point that the essential nature of ultimate reality transcends all opposites, all qualities and all concepts. In Bhagavad Gita, Krishna tells Arjuna that God cannot be described for He is without any qualities. God is above and beyond all thesis and antithesis: a synthesis that transcends all cycles of Hegelian dialectics. God is a subject for which there is no predicate.

Kena Upanishad says, "There the eye goes not,/ Speech goes not, nor the mind./ We know not, we understand not/ How would one teach it?" The ultimate spiritual reality transcends even the duality or dvaita of existence and non-existence, the opposites of being and non-being.

When we understand something intellectually, we do so in relation to something else. We do not know it intrinsically nor do we directly experience its innate essence. We identify the broader group it belongs to. Then we try to specify what makes it distinct from other members of the group. That is how we define anything.

How do we define a human being? We see that humans belong to the larger group of animals. We find that what distinguishes man from the rest of the animal kingdom is the fact that he is rational; so we conclude that man is a rational animal. The human mind pieces reality together by dissecting, differentiating and relating. Science tries to understand reality as a mechanism, taking apart its components and reassembling them.

According to modern physics, reality is fundamentally indivisible. It is inseparably interconnected as a cosmic web. The essence of reality, it turns out, is not mechanistic but metaphysical. Quantum physics has highlighted a fundamental limitation of the scientific method of understanding reality through observation and measurement. Einstein's theory has demonstrated that there is nothing absolute or immutable about a distance in space or a span of time.

Modern physics says that there is no such thing as an objective reality. An observer is not independent of the observation. The very act of observation affects what is observed. Consciousness too cannot detach itself from physical reality. Sri Aurobindo explained that the material object becomes "something different from what we now see, not a separate object on the background or in the environment of the rest of nature but an indivisible part and even in a subtle way an expression of the unity of all that we see".

Another way of understanding is through direct sensory experiencing. We understand pain as a sensation. We understand winter by experiencing the cold. We have to hoist ourselves out of the fundamental and circumscribing construct of our minds to stir ourselves in the profound spiritual depths of our being. The human mind discovers patterns among mentally stored abstractions of sensory experiences. It mechanically pieces together the jigsaw of physical reality through space and time sequences. We have to rise above this basic mental paradigm, which derives from the historical accumulation of man's sense perception, to become alive to the spiritual dimension.

The direct mystical experiencing of reality is non-sensory. As William James explains it, "Our normal waking consciousness, rational consciousness as we call it, is but one special type of consciousness, whilst all about it, parted from it by the flimsiest of screens, there lie potential forms of consciousness entirely different."

Enjoy Differences For Variety Spices Life

By Swami Sukhabodhananda

 young couple asked, "We have been married for several years but the only thing common between us is our irreconcilability. We are not able to make decisions; our indecisiveness is our common point. We don't even smile at each other. What do we do?" My response is simple: celebrate. Celebrate your differences. Make your differences fuel your togetherness. Just imagine how boring life would be if there were no differences.

Often people say they are upset that life is full of contradictions. Life is not so small that we can put it into compartments like good and bad, right and wrong, evil and noble. Life is vast; so vast that it is big enough to include contradictions in its fold.

The Kali symbol is a good illustration of this. Goddess Kali is shown dancing on the chest of her husband, Shiva. She loves her husband and, at the same time, dances on his chest, almost killing him. Life is full of contradictions. One has to accept them gracefully and, simultaneously, change whatever is possible. We also have to learn to accept what cannot be changed.

While we're discussing differences, let us accept that the context of a relationship should be one of love and not of expectation. Love has to go through transformation and purification. Only then would we find that we are bigger than our differences, and that we are slaves to differences.

Differences add richness, variety and spice to life. One should be creative in a relationship. In a music concert, there would be different musical instruments but all of them are harmonised to create symphony. The many tones, pitches and notes come together in a pleasing symphony. Exactly in the same way, you are different, your spouse is different. Learn to enjoy the differences.

The most important aspect in a relationship is that we should stand for transformation and growth. Transformation involves de-hypnotising ourselves. We are hypnotised into believing that love begins where differences end. Differences, in fact, add richness to life. The only thing one should be alert to is that differences should not be based on the ego; but on inner growth.

We can operate either from personality or from innocence. Personality comes from ego while innocence comes from a childlike nature. That which arises out of ego makes you feel heavy whereas what arises out of childlike innocence makes you feel light. When we are happy and pure and operate from innocence, our logic will have a different lustre, our understanding would have a different aura. It becomes divine. On the contrary, when we are impure and unhappy, our logic becomes dull and dry.

The greatest decision one has to make is the decision to be good, happy and helpful to humanity. In every organisation, it is important to take healthy decisions and create good discipline. This adds character to organisational culture. Enjoy life's differences and make decisions that take you closer to your destination:

"Life is an opportunity, cash in on it./ Life is an adventure, get into it./ Life is a tragedy, grow from it./ Life is a struggle, make it sacred./ Life is a song, sing it./ Life is a promise, meet it./ Life is a game, play it./ Life is a duty, fulfil it./ Life is a challenge, face it./ Life is a dream, realise it./ Life is beauty, feel it./ Life is bliss, experience it."

Individuals as Subsets of a Higher Set

By Rajesh B Pande

THE ultimate goal of the self-seeking is to unite with God. When a drop of water merges into the ocean, it loses its identity. The drop becomes part of a much larger whole. Much in the same way, individual souls seek union with God. There are different beliefs employing diverse practices to achieve this goal but, ultimately, it is only God's grace that helps us achieve success in this endeavour to merge with the Supreme One.

At the highest level, all existence is One. God is the highest level of our combined consciousness, also called the cosmic consciousness. Mathematically speaking, as individuals, we are subsets of a higher set.

Just as hundreds of terminals connected to a supercomputer seemingly work independently even though their actual control lies in the supercomputer, we, as individuals, may seem to have diametrically opposite personalities but the seeds of these traits spring from the same higher source. So, every one of us is connected in some way to the Supreme One.

The Big Bang created the material universe and, in the same way, eternally, the cosmic consciousness split itself up into different forms and levels. But this split does not mean that God has lost control. Far from it.

Due to the Big Bang, galaxies move away from each other and the universe is ever-expanding. But gravity is still in control and, after a critical time, everything will fall back as gravity draws the universe back to naught. This is the cycle of Creation. Just like the cycle of birth and death. In the same way, the superconsciousness will draw back all forms and levels of consciousness into itself.

In between these two events lies action—the zest for life, our worldly dreams, joy of achievement, tragedy of death, sacrifice of a messiah, treachery of a traitor—all of this impelled by a single life force.

Our sense of separateness from each other and from God is due to the fact that in our mental and sensory perceptions, we feel limited by our individual bodies. This is because we, as individuals, dwell at a much lower level of consciousness.

Each individual consciousness is bestowed with an ego, which makes it feel that it has an independent existence. It makes its own goals and lives its own life. But the source of all of its thoughts, aspirations and actions lies in the cosmic consciousness.

For some, the motivation may be to return to the source. Their endeavours in this direction may bear fruit, or may not, as the cosmic consciousness, the ultimate adjudicator, enjoys each of these trials and tribulations and decides the course. For those who fail, it is a Divine trial. For those who succeed, it is a gift, the grace of God. God motivates, guides and performs through us.

Many people have achieved realisation through different methods that seem philosophically paradoxical. Yet the end result is the same for all of them. This is because the secret of a realised soul does not lie in the methods chosen but in the grace of God.

No methods, no meditation, no prayer can make one eligible for union with God. It's only when God yearns for us and we yearn for God, we will be called. Till then, we can only wait and play out our roles as best as we can in this cosmic drama.

Why You Shouldn't Look For Superhumans in Avatars

Discourse: Sri Sri Ravishankar

IFE is incomplete without union with God. It is quite natural that a matured mind and a receptive heart strive for this union. Since long, philosophies were born, debates happened, music, art and literature evolved from this very need. Religions, philosophies, practices, customs and austerities have all pointed to one thing: union with the Divine.

On an average, the person who wakes up to suffering in his life wants to be free from it. For this, he looks to the superpower of creation. The more he looks at the misery and shortcomings in his life, the farther away he feels from the Divinity which is his very nature. His heart yearns to establish contact with the Supreme.

Since ages, we've been striving to reduce the gap between ourselves and God. There are two ways to do this: one way is to elevate humankind towards Divinity—this is called Siddha, and the person who achieves this state is believed to have attained perfection. The second way is to bring God to human level in avatar form. Here, Divinity manifests itself for the sake of humankind. So, man rising up to God is Siddha; God coming down, because he cares for you, and wants to communicate directly with you, is avatar.

Avatar is God in human form, and in that human-ness, you can get a glimpse of Divinity. In the Puranas, all the devas are depicted with human emotions and tendencies. They experience "normal" feelings of anger, love and resentment.

Rama and Krishna went through a gamut of human experience in order to make us realise that God need not be a distant concept: God can be one among us. So, don't look for the superhuman in an avatar.

The concept of avatar is common in the East in countries like India, China, Japan, Korea and Nepal. "Nripo Narayano Hari": the king is regarded as the avatar of Vishnu. "Vaidhyo Narayano Hari": the doctor, too, is venerated as Vishnu-avatar. In the West, the Divine Messenger aids spiritual evolution. In the East, there is greater intimacy between humans and God. Hence, the avatar is like a mother going personally to her child; there is greater emotional bonding.

Spiritual evolution through heartfelt, personal devotion is typically eastern, whereas the western perspective is based on the concept of a messenger and, hence, is necessarily more formal. The bhaktas and Sufis were more comfortable with the idea of avatar. For an intimate relationship, God comes directly. Your love for God becomes authentic when you are assured of His love for you. In Bhagavad Gita, it is Krishna who first tells Arjuna: "You are dear to me", which enabled Arjuna to surrender.

Wherever you feel immense respect, wherever you get a glimpse of Divinity, know that it is avatar. Avatar lies in those who recognise—and entire creation comes alive as Divinity. This is the stage before the awareness of "I Am".

The entire phenomenon of creation is the descent of consciousness in various names and forms. The whole purpose of avatar is to make you realise that you are part of Him. Avatar is not there to charm you but to calm you; to make you return home. And to make you realise you are that. Once you recognise the avatar, suddenly, the entire creation is filled with "that" and you are that. The descent of God is to make you realise that there is neither up nor down. There is no high or low, ascension or descent.

Swami Vivekananda: The Manager Monk

By Anshul Chaturvedi

N an age when 30-something CEOs and VPs no longer surprise us and paradigms are busted each day, holding one's own at the workplace is a challenge in itself. One hundred and forty-one years after Swami Vivekananda was born, we need to evoke his vision and focus on the fact that life at the workplace can be much simpler and more fulfilling.

The Swami may not have been a student of management theory but the fundamental truths that he taught are invaluable in today's globalised workplace, where employees are often resentful of the relative success of others.

Talk of cultivating a spiritual approach at the time of annual increments might give rise to cynicism among some, but it is in tune with Vivekananda's thoughts: "We find ourselves in the position for which we are fit... if one has some capacity above another, the world will find it out too... He who grumbles at the little thing that has fallen to his lot to do, will grumble at everything. Always grumbling, he will lead a miserable life... But that man who does his duty as he goes, putting his shoulder to the wheel, higher and higher duties will fall to his share."

Wondering what the top bosses do with the astronomical sums they take home may be good for office chit-chat but it isn't of much help in getting to where they are. Vivekananda's analysis of how the hierarchy works can help us to assess our progress without regrets: "No man can long occupy satisfactorily a position for which he is not fit. By doing well the duty which is nearest to us, the duty which is in our hands now, we make ourselves stronger; and improving our strength in this manner we may even reach a state in which it shall be our privilege to do the most coveted and honoured duties in life and in society."

If we take a random look at those doing the "most coveted duties"—whether it is a Narayana Murthy or Amitabh Bachchan—we will find that they are people who did well the duty that was nearest to them at any given point of time; that is all that we need to do.

Equally, there is little sense in being aggrieved when one feels that someone else has been elevated to a role beyond his competence. Even for the highest offices, the rule that "no man can long occupy satisfactorily a position for which he is not fit" has held true repeatedly; it is not difficult to find instances of former prime ministers who have faded into obscurity. If a person is not equipped to handle a role and make a mark at the job, it does not take long for that to be obvious.

An organisational weakness is that issues are often soft-pedalled when personal equations come into play. But Vivekananda advises us to put aside such hesitations where professional issues are concerned: "All-combined India sinks under efforts in the weight of one iniquity—we have not developed strict business principles." Business is business, and no friendship should be used to subvert this.

"Let the world say what it chooses, I shall tread the path of duty... Otherwise, if one has to attend day and night to what this man says or that man writes, no great work is achieved in this world," said the Swami.

His profound thoughts continue to inspire thousands even a century after his demise, though he lived for barely four decades. Stephen Covey might be the current must-read but Vivekananda could well lay claim to being the original proponent of the character ethic.

An American's Love For Durga

By M N Chatterjee

ANNE Lowenkopf, a California-based American writer, finds Devi Mahatmyam not only relevant but also inspirational in the present age. Of particular interest to her is the following portion of the Sanskrit hymns which recount the heroic exploits of Devi Durga while overpowering the rampaging asuras: "I am all alone in the world here. Who else is there besides me? See these goddesses who are but my own powers entering into my own self."

Anne finds the Mother Goddess to be all-encompassing. According to her, the vision of the loving and protective mother excites attention today when more and more young adults live alone, outside family and organised peer groups. They seem to feel close to a deity who, in turn, gives them unconditional love and comfort. Single adults and the young raised by them—who have to face difficulties single-handedly—are quick to appreciate a goddess who copes with danger all by herself. In Anne's words, "This concept of the Mother first attracted me as a young woman rebelling against the notion of being born in need of redemption for the action of others." She is thrilled at her discovery of a "Goddess who did not punish the created for what went wrong in her creation, who took the heat for evil and death and yet was untouched by both." She narrates an incident in which an American—brought up in the climate of Victorian notions of maternal behaviour—asked a contemporary devotee of the Devi how he could be drawn to such a fierce goddess. He was told: "Ah, but you need a strong mother who will go to battle for you when you are in trouble."

Shankaracharya sang the Mother Goddess's praise thus: "Immersed in dangers, O Durga, I turn my mind to you, O Ocean of Mercy and spouse of Shiva; please don't consider this as my deceit, since children remember their mother when they suffer from hunger and thirst." In Soundarya Lahari, he underscores Her unique power in the following words: "If Shiva is united with Shakti, He becomes capable of being almighty; if not, He is not even able to move His limbs." There may be a bad son, he says, but never a bad mother.

Vedanta gives the mother a cosmic dimension as Jagdamba. As Para Shakti or the embodiment of infinite energy, she is also Para Prakriti, bountiful nature, nourishing us. She symbolises the rationale for ecological balance and fruitful coexistence. The shakti-pithas, the holy spots, which are centres of pilgrimage, are a testimony to the symbiotic ties between the Mother Goddess and Mother Earth. These places are where various parts of her body fell when being carried away by an enraged Shiva, who suffered humiliation at the hands of Daksha, Shakti's father.

The 700-verse Devi Mahatmyam, which is a part of Markandeya Purana, is also called Chandi. Its recitation is called Chandipath, an essential part of the invocation, for the puja. It narrates the story of Devi Durga, Her origin and Her militant role as the deliverer. It depicts the plight of the helpless gods, harried by the demon, Mahishasura, and his ilk, and narrates how Devi Chandika was born of divine energy to challenge the might of the asuras. She had female helpers, Matrikas or mothers, on the battleground. The Shakti cult was later influenced by the Vaishnavite version of the return of the beloved daughter to Her maternal home in the plains from Her home in the Himalayas. Vijaya Dashami marks the day of Her departure to Her home and spouse.

A Tale of Two Yogis: Yogananda & Babaji

By D K Sharma

PARAMHANSA Yogananda talked about Mahavatar Babaji for the first time in his Autobiography of a Yogi. Also known as Nagraj Babaji, Mahavatar Baba had Tamil origins. His followers believe he is approximately 1,000 years old. Babaji's disciples think of him as the incarnation of Lord Shiva, and so believe that he is present everywhere. Babaji once told his disciples of the Creator: "He is deathless. He can do whatever He wills. The whole universe is an expanded bubble ready to burst before Him." A Mahayogi himself, Babaji is said to have spent centuries as a recluse in the Himalayas, performing intense penance and meditation to attain enlightenment. Many of his disciples believe that the Mahavatar moves around in the interior recesses of the Himalayas accompanied by a group of highly evolved American, European and Indian disciples. Seldom was Mahavatar Babaji spoken of earlier, because of his self-negating approach to enlightenment.

Mahavatar Babaji pioneered Kriya Yoga, the form of yoga envisioned by Krishna in Bhagavad Gita. Far removed from the mundane, Babaji believed that the yogi must allow his consciousness to expand to be "undifferentiated" with the Almighty who is the "Ultimate Reality". Self-dedication is surrendering the ego and loving humankind. Selfless service is service performed with detachment, without expecting returns. To attain this, Babaji put forth five major kriya yogas: hatha yoga, kundalini pranayam, dhyanasana, mantra yoga and bhakti yoga. If Patanjali, who wrote the Yoga Sutra nearly 2,005 years ago, was instrumental in defining the principles of yoga in its different forms, Paramhansa Yogananda played a major role in popularising those principles worldwide. Mahavatar was a siddha sadhaka, a saint who attained realisation of the Supreme.

Kri means action and ya means awareness. So kriya means action through awareness. Yoga unites the individual self with the cosmic self through expansion of consciousness. The yogi controls breath, channelises his energy to revolve upwards and downwards around the six spinal centres and, thus, spiritually magnetises his body cells. Half-a-minute of kriya equals a year of a natural spiritual hug. The Kriya Yogi arrests the deterioration of body capacity by infusing an additional supply of prana (life force) through quietening of actions of lungs and heart. He neutralises decay and growth, and learns how the life force is controlled.

Krishna depicted how desire, fear and anger can be banished through a sensory mode, gazing. The non-flinching gaze has magical effects. The guru's fixed gaze upon the middle point of eyebrows of the disciple will exude a tremendous healing force. This can also be attained by neutralising the current of prana and aprana (devoid of the life force) within the nostrils and lungs.

Saint-writer Yogananda mentioned that Babaji had initiated Adi Shankaracharya and mediaeval saint-poet Kabir into Kriya Yoga. In the phantasmagorial world of the siddha sadhaka, a Kriya Yoga exponent is capable of taking various shapes—through the process of transformation—as a tree, swan, bird, animal, or any other living being. He can even become invisible. Life becomes a wilful expanse for the yogi and distance is not an eventual reality. Some Kriya Yogis transport themselves as beams of light. Babaji advocated attainment of soruba samadhi. It is another form of high yoga in which an individual surrenders to the Divine Will and allows that Will to transform his human nature.

Divine Import of Krishna Leela

By Ashutosh Ji Maharaj

T was the darkest hour of the era. The brutalities perpetrated by despot king Kansa had become unbearable. In such a period of crisis, during the Dwapar Yuga, the Divine Power descended on earth in human form as Krishna. He is Raagi as well as Vairaagi; Nar and Narayan; Chakradhar and Murlidhar—all blending into one incarnation, Krishna. Even the pranks and adventures of Balakrishna and his friends had subtle transcendental messages. Stealing butter from homes, Krishna as makhanchor points out the dualistic nature of the world. This world is an amalgamation of the essential (butter) and the non-essential (buttermilk). By relishing butter, Krishna inspires us to abstract the Supreme Essence, mayapati, and enjoy pure bliss. Likewise, the sport of trampling over the poisonous hoods of serpent Kalia is also quite figurative. A similar kind of venomous snake is hissing within us. It is our conceited mind. The mind, through its attachment to sensuous desires, incessantly poisons the inner-self. Krishna's feat on the banks of the Yamuna symbolises the initiation of Brahma-Jnana within us. Experiencing the Divine through this knowledge will help us overcome vice. Such a pure heart then proves out to be a perfect platform for Krishna's dance of victory.

Krishna Leela is both divine and transcendental. But many fail to understand its real import. This failure, in turn, gives rise to innumerable doubts and even leads to vehement protests objecting to Krishna's leelas—like the rasleela between Krishna and the gopis. Krishna then was hardly 7-8 years old and the gopikas were much older. Moreover, rasleela was in reality bhavleela, completely devoid of corporeal sensations. It was the celestial, atmic form of a gopi that used to participate in ras. Far above the carnal plane, it was a divine communion between souls (gopis) and the Supreme Soul (Krishna). Krishna Leela is Eko Aham Bahusyama, One manifested as Many.

Critics also condemn Krishna's role in the battle of Kurukshetra. They argue that Krishna, with his divine powers, could have prevented the war from taking place. Moreover, they point out, Krishna adopted unrighteous means to slay many great warriors of the Kauravas. But the Mahabharata war cannot be analysed like this in isolation—one has to take note of the larger picture. When a limb gets infected and is beyond repair, and there is danger of the patient losing his life because of this, the surgeon has no option left but to amputate the infected limb. The Kauravas posed a real threat to society. They, in fact, had turned murderous—they did not hesitate to set aflame the Lakshagriha where the Pandavas were staying; they aided and abetted the disrobing of Draupadi; they rejected all peace proposals by Krishna and were reluctant to offer even five villages to resolve the dispute. They preferred to go to battle.

To infer and gain knowledge from the divine actions of incarnations, we need divine vision. This is what Krishna revealed to Arjuna: "What thou hast to see, thy human eye cannot grasp; but there is a divine eye and that I now give to thee. Behold Me in my Divine Yoga." On attaining the divine eye, Arjuna could see the cosmic form of Krishna. Then only could he know the divine nature of Krishna. Janmashtami celebrates the spirit of Krishna, and reiterates the need to cultivate Krishna consciousness and to make efforts to realise Krishna in His elemental form through Brahma-Jnana.

A Temple For the Goddess of Animal

By K M Gupta

OME way off the old Calicut-Madras Trunk Road there is a village called Thachanattukara. And in this village, there is a temple dedicated to Jyeshta, the goddess of misfortune. It is the only one of its kind in the whole of India.

Jyeshta in feminine gender means "elder sister". She is the elder sister of Mahalakshmi, the goddess of good fortune. While Lakshmi is the goddess of riches, her elder sister is the deity of poverty, indigence, odium, reproach and ignominy. Her very name is a term of reproach. Lakshmi is the idol of the auspicious and the propitious, of all that is desirable in life, whereas her sister, Jyeshta, is the symbol of all that is detestable, damnable and loathsome. The two sisters are born rivals. Where one is in, the other is out.

The Indian household is engaged in a constant fight to keep Lakshmi in and Jyeshta out. Waste, dirt, squalor, slovenliness, indolence, idleness, disorder, anger and all such undesirable things show the presence of Jyeshta in the house. Until she is turned out, Lakshmi wouldn't enter and stay. In some houses, it is a custom for the lady of the house to open the back door first, send Jyeshta out and then open the front door and let Lakshmi in. Once Lakshmi and Jyeshta stood at the doorstep quarrelling over which one of them was more beautiful. When the householder appeared, the two sisters asked him to be the judge. The clever householder, wary of displeasing either of them, hedged: "You, Lakshmi, are more beautiful when you enter, and you, Jyeshta, are more beautiful when you exit." Both were pleased. Lakshmi entered the house and Jyeshta exited proudly.

Lakshmi is Sridevi, the goddess of the blessed, and Jyeshta is Moodevi, the goddess of the accursed and the damned. Then how is it that this persona non grata among the Hindu pantheon was able to find a house of worship for her in Thachanattukara? Lakshmi is known to be chanchala—unsteady and fleeting. She is also dukhamoola—the cause of misery and misfortune. Lakshmi is the source of happiness only in appearance. In truth, underneath, she is the source of misery. The fight for Lakshmi moolah (dukhamoola) debases and often inhumanises man. The world loves and worships Lakshmi because it is cursed to love and worship appearance. Lakshmi is the goddess of appearance. Jyeshta is poor and indigent, but she has strength of character. She is not chanchala. She is not seductive. She discounts appearance. She is steady and unflinching. She has grit. It is the strength of the soul that gives man real strength and happiness, not moolah. Beneath the level of appearance, Jyeshta is the giver of real strength and happiness.

Actually, the roles of Lakshmi and Jyeshta are interchanged. In the deep spiritual sense, Lakshmi is Jyeshta and Jyeshta is Lakshmi. The wise worship Jyeshta, not Lakshmi. Lakshmi is the goddess of persona and Jyeshta is the deity of anima. Jyeshta has no worshippers in the world because the world worships only persona or appearance and glamour and not anima or inner soul. The Jyeshta temple in Thachanattukara is a unique symbol of the Indian psyche, which is non-exclusive by nature. Hence, it is the "Hindu Sphinx" to the West. India's Sanatana Dharma is, in fact, a miniature representation of nature: "All In, Naught Out". In nature, everything has its role and place. So is it in Sanatana Dharma. It accommodates all. It expands to take up all. It extends from advaita to the most grotesque forms of worship. It extends from dhyana to animal sacrifice. It ranges from passionate bhakti to arch atheism. It extends from the worship of Lakshmi to the worship of Jyeshta. The Jyeshta shrine is a fine symbolism of India's anima.

Prince of Ayodhya, Prophet of Peace

By S Ragi Simhan

AMA is an avatar of Maha Vishnu. He is the Adi Purush—the Ancient One—who, out of compassion for humankind, descends to Earth in human form, taking upon himself the trials and tribulations of human existence, willingly suffering ordeals to protect the virtuous and annihilate the wicked. Indeed, the Ramavatara is one of the most splendid of Maha Vishnu's manifestations in order to redeem His pledge to "appear in bodily forms whenever virtue decays and evil causes misery to the good and the virtuous, and the earth itself" (Sant Tulsidas).

Maha Vishnu's innumerable qualities defy description and His energy pervades the whole cosmos. Whether sporting with prakriti, primordial matter, or playfully performing his numerous lilas, He as the Lord of the past, present and future, assumes the form of the Trinity—Brahma, Vishnu and Shiva—to create, sustain and dissolve creation that emanates from Him and merges into Him. From His Consciousness emerges knowledge of the Vedas, Yoga, Sankhya, sciences, architecture, the 64 human perfections, scriptures and the ultimate wisdom of seeking one's true Self.

Sages of yore, from revelations that came through intense meditation, gathered a thousand namas or names for Maha Vishnu, each as Sri Ramanujacharya explained, containing a hundred meanings expounding the quintessence of the Supreme Being. These are called the Sri Vishnu Sahasranama. In the Mahabharata, Bhishma, awaiting death on a bed of arrows, revealed the esoterics of the namas to Yudhishtira. Part of the revelation was that meditating on the essence of each nama frees one from fear and sins and leads to the Lord's perennial grace.

Parvati once asked Lord Shiva the way to attain Maha Vishnu, who was beyond comprehension. Shiva, with delightful simplicity, answered that by meditating on the sweet name of Sri Rama, one attained blissful union with the "Immaculate One" as the persona of Sri Rama embodied the Vishnu Sahasranama. According to Tulsidas, the two syllables of Sri Rama's name, "ra" and "ma", are like the sound of a clap that drives away birds of doubt, leading to unclouded faith in the redeeming nature of the Divine.

One realises the truth of this when reading, hearing, singing or seeing an enactment of the Ramayana. The emotions it invokes within one range from excruciating sorrow to the sublime, from the ennobling to the enlightening, ending in a truly humbling experience. Faith in Sri Rama, an embodiment of dharma, thus translates into peace, happiness and true wisdom.

The Ramayana, first and foremost, expounds dharma, the Universal Law, which for every individual, translates into conquering the enemies—lust, anger and greed. In Sundar Kand, a brahmastra-bound Hanuman advises Ravana to return Sita or face ruin at the hands of Sri Rama. He tells Ravana that although the power to do good or evil equally stem from dharma, he who commits evil strikes at the root of his freedom of choice, inviting upon himself sure death—the truth which Ravana realises only too late.

The Ramayana is as much a guide to right living for the commoner as it is for the rulers. The epic emphasises rajdharma, that, rulers can never be above the law but must forever sacrifice their personal interests, their paramount consideration being only the welfare of the state and all its citizens. Secondly, the Ramayana tells the story of God taking the form of a human being who has full control over his senses and leads a life as ordained by the scriptures, teachings of seers and in keeping with his conscience. One among Vishnu's thousand names is Samukhaya nama—the One with the beautiful face. Illustrating the Vedic injunction that one must lead a life of detachment with serenity, neither over-reacting to the pleasant nor bemoaning pain, Kamban, the great Tamil poet, taking a cue from this nama, describes Sri Rama upon hearing Kaikeyi's harsh words: "That beautiful face which, both when asked by his father to accept the imperial crown as well as when commanded by his mother to leave all and live in a forest, like the pictorial lotus, was ever the same." (V V S Aiyar's Kamba Ramayana.) Indeed, Sri Rama is an exemplar, the Maryada Purushottam and his thoughts, acts and deeds are a guide to human beings effectively realising the four Purusharths—dharma, artha, kama and moksha (true faith, economic well-being, sensual enjoyment and spiritual salvation).

Situation Vacant: Saviour Wanted

By Aruna Jethwani

"THE world is in flames. Quench it with the waters of the spirit," remarked an Indian sage. He might have foreseen that one day, even the eastern hemisphere, despite its wealth of wisdom, would not be spared. And so it has come to pass. This is evident in India, where the flames of anger and despair have left both the innocent and the not-so-innocent smouldering in a volcanic lava. When the inferno is over—it could be Gujarat or Kashmir—it will leave mounds of ashes and heaps of soot. Who will sweep them? Who will clean up afterwards? Who will quench the thirst of a bloodthirsty people? Will a messiah pass this way? We need rejuvenation. This rejuvenation will come only with the revival of our great ideals. We need shakti. For this, extensive rebuilding needs to be initiated for the people to acquire physical, mental and spiritual strength. For creating this stupendous energy, we need a new spiritual awakening. A new direction. The inspiration for such an awakening could come from a prophet of peace, for instance, someone like Guru Nanak, who proclaimed: "Love the saints of every faith /Put away the pride! /The essence of religion is /Humility, service, and sympathy. /Not fine clothes, /Not the yogi's garb and ashes, /Not the blowing of horn /Not the shaven head, /Not long prayers..." It was this spirit of equality which attracted devotees from all faiths, who flocked to hear and follow Guru Nanak's teachings.

Sufis like Shah Abdul Latif and Jalal'uddin Rumi—with a secularist vision—could bring about a synthesis of various religions and schools of thought. To a Sufi, everything is beauty, and he sees that beauty in all humanity—free from caste, creed or colour. Sachal, a Sindh Sufi saint, wrote this poem: "Hindus and Muslims /Are all emanations /Of the one name—Aliph! /Burn the books to ashes and dust /Thus hath the Murshid taught me! /He too hath taught me /To know the eternal! /To every one of you I say, /Thou must first know thyself, /Then walk the way of love!" It would be wonderful indeed if we could somehow recall these enlightened Sufi saints to contemporary times.

India needs a saint-poet like Kabir, a person who could weave the message of the importance of unity into simple verses: "Neither Guru nor chela I am /Neither Murshid nor Pir /I am neither the one not the other /Sitting tight I am Kabir!..." In another verse, he sang: "At death Hindus chant the name of Lord Rama, /Muslims chant Khuda's name /In their lifetime neither of them /Does ever chant the same."

Sai Baba of Shirdi professed neither caste nor religion. He believed in love for mankind. It is said about Mughal emperor Akbar that he was a perfect king. He married a Hindu Rajput woman, Jodhabai; observed Hindu festivals and on matters of state, consulted Hindus as well as Muslims. But the urgent need today is for someone like Emperor Ashoka since he progressed from violence to compassion, from cruelty to mercy, from turmoil to peace, from destruction to construction, from death to life, from ego to egolessness, from the unreal to ultimate reality. Sadhu Vaswani said: "We stand in need of great architects for the building of a new India. The first I call the seer or the rishi. The second architect is the leader. The third architect is the social servant/teacher. The fourth, men of sympathy, love and sacrifice, who would rise above their selfish ego and empathise with the people." Is there anyone out there who can fulfil the requirements of a potential saviour?

A Glowing Tribute To the Tenth Guru

By Patwant Singh

IKHISM'S astonishing appeal lies in the degree to which Sikhs draw strength from it. Besides providing a bedrock of religious beliefs—which sustain them in their journey through life—this youngest of the six great faiths also stresses the importance of defining an individual's ethical and humane basis for existence. Its ten Gurus or teachers emphasised the need to expand those elements of the spirit which enable people to be more complete in themselves, to develop a sense of existential purpose, the confidence to achieve the impossible, a capacity for compassion, a philosophic acceptance of life's ups and downs.

The individual's moral fibre had to be strengthened through basic convictions. With this farsightedness, the tenth and last Guru, Gobind Singh, set about honing the faith's dynamics through innovation and personal example. His rigorous self-discipline and inner fortitude were exemplified by his equanimity and poise in the face of tragedies few encounter in their lifetime. He was nine when he received the head of his father Guru Tegh Bahadur, beheaded in Delhi on the orders of the Mughal Emperor, Aurangzeb. His father had chosen martyrdom to demonstrate that a man convinced of his moral purpose and inalienable right to practise his faith, is unafraid to die. The spiritual significance of his father's bold and assertive defiance of the imperium, which denied its subjects their essential rights and freedoms, was not lost on young Gobind, and his conduct during the next 33 years, between the age of nine, when his father died, and his death at the age of 42, shows how the concept of martyrdom shaped his character. J D Cunningham, an official of the East India Company and author of a classic history of the Sikhs, describes his contribution: "In the heart of a powerful empire he set himself to the task of subverting it, and from the midst of social degradation and religious corruption he called up simplicity of manners, singleness of purpose, and enthusiasm."

Convinced that only people with an iron will and high self-esteem could oppose injustice, he laid the foundation of martial traditions so his people could proudly proclaim their beliefs and moral goals. He baptised them as a first step towards giving them a distinct identity. In a simple ceremony, an iron bowl full of clear water with sugar added, was stirred by a double-edged sword and a few drops of this magical mix of sweetness and steel—called amrit—were administered to the thousands waiting on the day of Baisakhi in April 1699. He called baptised Sikhs, the Khalsa: a people distinctive in appearance, completely equal, with shared ideals, principles and sense of purpose, without caste distinctions and with service or sewa of humanity as an article of their faith. It would be the most democratic of all faiths. The sword—in effect, steel—became the symbol of their pride and purpose and of the divine being's will by which the Khalsa would raise it to defend the defenceless and its own beliefs.

Bhai Gurdas, a chronicler of the Gurus, places the Khalsa's emphasis on military preparedness in this perspective: "The orchard of the Sikh faith needed the thorny hedge of armed men for its protection." Military skill was just one facet of Guru Gobind Singh's personality. He also learnt Sanskrit, Braj, Persian, Arabic and Avadhi, and studied the classics in these languages. These scholarly foundations resulted in a book of psalms, a narrative of his times, an autobiography, the inclusion of his father's hymns in the Guru Granth Sahib—the sacred writings of the Sikhs—and poems based on the entire gamut of human existence. The diversity of the Guru's interests ranged from astronomy, geography, metaphysics, yoga and botany to Ayurvedic healing. Because of the wide range of his interests and his all-embracing vision, he rose above the petty prejudices of his time to become an uncompromising advocate of humanistic principles. He stressed this ethic in his poetic composition, Akal Ustat: "Recognise all mankind as one,/ Whether Hindus or Muslims,/ The same Lord is the creator/ and nourisher of all:/ Recognise no distinction between them./ The monastery and the mosque are the same,/ So is Hindu worship and Muslim prayer./ Men are all one!" His life is a telling reaffirmation of his personal values. Despite the fact that his great-grandfather, father, four sons and countless comrades-in-arms were put to death by those in power, he opposed no faith or its followers, but only the tyrannical few who denied others the right to practise their beliefs.

A Kondh's Love For Life and Dharani

By Sitakant Mahapatra

HE hill-stream gurgled along impatiently. The old Kondh tribal sat by the stream, both feet dipped into its cold waters. The blue smoke from the home-made pipe he was smoking merged with the blue haze slowly descending from the Niyamgiri hill. Soon he was playing a wistful tune on a slender flute. The music drew me to him and we started talking. He told me how he lost his wife a year ago. "The tiger dragged her away while she was in the forest. I was so unhappy I wanted to die and leave Dharani Ma (Earth Mother). Then deep inside I knew I couldn't, unless forced, leave this enchanting world even for a day. This world of beautiful hill-streams, forest, trees, bird-songs, parabs (festivals), the handia (local liquor made from rice gruel), the beautiful aroma of roasted meat, the moonlit nights, the songs and dances of dhangdas and dhangdis (unmarried boys and girls), the golden mustard fields extending right up to the hills and, above all, this flute music."

The Kondh tribal was 75, shrivelled, sinewy and ancient-looking but he was smiling. He persuaded me to visit his village just a slope away. I noticed at the village akhra (meeting ground/dance-floor), the succession list of eleven saontas, village headmen, each with a pointed stone. So I knew the village was eleven generations old. On the way up the hill, my stay and return the next day, I kept asking myself: "What made this man so deeply wedded to life?" Despite his sorrow, he said: "If some day I leave this world I would like to come back here, return again and again and again and I would persuade my wife to follow me here." And so I knew for him there is rebirth, but he would like to return only to his known and intimate world. "My ancestors' bones are below its soil. It is sacred," he explained.

I remembered this line from Madhusudan Stotra: "O Madhusudan save me as I do not intend to come back yet again!" What a sharp contrast in points of view, the attitude to life! One speaks wearily of getting born and reborn in this world, of the ongoing cycle of birth and death; most crave for release from the cycle.

Adi Sankara, too, had spoken of the "ignorance" of not realising that we all undergo the cycle of birth and death. He composed the Bhaja Govindam and Smara Govindam on this theme. To wish to come back to life on earth, how intense must be one's love for life! We will never know what made the old

Kondh of Niyamgiri say that; to yearn to come back to Dharani Ma, preferably with his wife, back to the same place. Each individual must find his reasons or lack of it for such feelings. But to love life one must intensely love this world and all its men, forests, rivers, valleys, everything. Nazim Hikmet wrote: "This earth will grow cold one day,/ not like a block of ice/ or a dead cloud even/ but like an empty walnut/ in pitch-black space;/ you must grieve for it right now/ you have to feel this sorrow now/ for the world must be loved this much." Such an intense love for the world is born out of a deep realisation within. Not so much in the brain cells as in the heart; not the intellect but the instinctive emotion; the realisation that the umbilical cord connects each of us to life on this planet. German poet Rilke said as much as the Niyamgiri Kondh, only differently: "Once and no more. And we too/ once. And never again; But this/ having been once, though only once/ having been once on earth/ can it ever be cancelled?"

When Chaplin Got Convinced of Gandhi's Philosophy

By Amrit Gangar

 meeting of Charlie Chaplin with Mahatma Gandhi in a humble little house—in the slum district off the East India Dock Road—in London was brief but significant. At the end of this meeting, Gandhi explained to Chaplin the true meaning of supreme independence. It was to shed oneself of unnecessary things. This was in the context of Gandhiji's astute political-economic-spiritual theory that Chaplin presumed was against the use of machinery.

What Gandhi told Chaplin that day, on September 22, 1931 echoes the Jaina principle of aparigraha. Gandhi was deeply influenced by the principle of Jainism.

Simply put, aparigraha means non-possession or non-acquisition. If you need two shirts, don't go in for the third one. It is sacrificing the superfluous consumption of a "one more". However, the dialectical history of the human mind has proved to be more complex and intractable than it appears to be.

In the context of globalisation, the applied theory of aparigraha could be a good interventionist tool besides being a crucial ecological arm to help retain the essential balance between man and nature to make a sustainable future possible. Gandhi knew its value, both strategically and spiritually. He was a practising environmentalist, long before environmental protection became fashionable. Gandhi provided us a vikalp, an alternative model of development.

One of the five basic Jaina principles—followed by both monks and the laity—is aparigraha, a realistic, practical and rational concept that can contribute to a society's stability. Its main thrust is on a balanced society with balanced individuals. This secular principle does not allow greed to dominate our thoughts and actions and can help us overcome the tendency to accumulate.

Practical wisdom tells us that anything in excess is bad. Over-consumption, over-possession, and over-acquisition all affect our social environment just as environmental degradation affects our physical survival. Aparigraha can be practised by preserving nature, conserving energy and living austerely. It is all about creating well-being through moderation and balance. Inequity in the world today is alarming. Over the past four years the world's 200 richest people have doubled their wealth to more than one trillion US dollars while 1.3 billion people are living on less than a dollar a day.

Jainism believes that the more worldly wealth a person possesses, the more he is likely to commit sin and he may be more unhappy. Worldly wealth creates attachments and greed, jealousy, selfishness, ego, hatred and violence.

Right knowledge, right faith and right conduct are the three basic essentials for attaining liberation. To acquire these, Jainism prescribes observation of the five great vows: ahimsa or non-violence, satya or truth, asteya or non-stealing, brahmacharya or celibacy, and aparigraha or non-possession/non-attachment. Happiness is about freedom from pain and this is possible only by leading a life of simplicity and non-attachment.

The essence of aparigraha is that "less" actually yields "more"—more peace and happiness from consuming less. In short, simple living and high thinking, as the Mahatma would have put it.

Music-Bhakti Combination Is Vital For Moksha

By Indira Menon

YAGARAJA had surrendered himself, body and soul, to Rama. He dedicated his works to Him. However, he never attempted to narrate the Ramayana in his song-compositions though there are innumerable references to it. In fact, he has invoked various other deities as well though they are far less in number. He does not figure among the bhakti saints. It is as a vaggeyakara that Tyagaraja has attained immortality. The universality of his themes has a special appeal. His music goes straight to the heart. Pain, suffering, anguish, joy, ecstasy, and the eternal quest for the ultimate, all universal emotions, find an outlet in it.

For Tyagaraja music was supreme. His kritis show that his works are a celebration of music itself. No composer has addressed himself to the art per se, to the presence of divinity in music. There are compositions dedicated to the goddess of arts and learning, Saraswati, but none to the art of music. He refers to the seven notes as beautiful goddesses who preside over music that emanates from the nabhi and travels up to the heart, throat, lips, and nose. The nectar of ragas yields the fruits of yaga, yoga, tyaga and bhoga—so partake of it with joy, he says, in Ragasudharasa. Knowledge about the resonant sthanas of the saptaswaras will grant moksha or Swararagasudharasa.

Tyagaraja believed that his music was of divine origin. In his kritis there are repeated references to the sage Narada, and to the Swararnavam, a treatise on musicology in the form of a dialogue between Shiva and Parvati—a part of the larger work, Swararagasudharasa—which, he said, was presented to him by Narada himself.

In the centre of the body is the life-breath; in the centre of the life-breath is sound; in the centre of sound is musical sound; in the centre of musical sound is godhead. That the body is a temple of music is brought out in the kriti Mokshamugalada. The fusion of life-breath and fire—prananala samyogamu—produces the primordial sound, OM or Pranavanada, which is the basis of the saptaswara. Tyagaraja refers to the mooladhara from where nada emerges and travels up the chakras of the spine taking the jeevanmukta towards moksha.

Did Tyagaraja choose music as the vehicle of Rama worship? Or was it the other way round? Did he use the Rama metaphor to experiment with his musical ideas? In sheer ecstatic joy he even suggests that Rama incarnated Himself to bless him for his kirtanas composed in the garland of gem-like ragas (Elavathara). For, he believed that without bhakti one cannot achieve heights of excellence in music and, through music, salvation—"Sangita jnanamu bhaktivina sanmargamu galade o manasa."

There is no moksha for those devoid of music. Those who do not float on the ocean of bliss that is sangita are a burden on earth, "bhoobharamu" (Anandasagarame). But those who do shall not only receive divine grace—sarupya saukhya—but also other benefits such as love, bhakti, vatsalya and blessings of the Lord. If knowledge of music without bhakti does not lead one to bliss, the obverse is also true. Bhakti saturated with the nectar of swara and raga is the sure path to paradise.

Experience the Mystic Resonance of Voice

By Bindu Chawla

N its pure state, the human voice is an expression of the divine. Forever rooted in the naada or cosmic sound through the naabhi or navel, the voice, when activated, is a manifestation, aahada naada or heard sound of the Unmanifest, anahada naada or unheard sound.

Yet, the connection may be veiled by many years, even births, of "false" conditioning. When we perform sadhana of any kind, cleansing and purifying the mind, we restore, as it were, the transparency of this connection. The story of naada yoga or the yoga of sound is the story of a return to the naabhi swara, the voice of truth, qalab ki aawaaz, that speaks straight from the soul.

In the vocal tradition of the Indore gharana of the Hindustani khayal, Pandit Amarnath's teaching centred around this journey, of a return of the voice to its own "root", to aawaaz ki "jad" pakadnaa. And with that, to a singing which celebrated this return.

The first steps involved "opening" the voice, "aawaaz kholna", for at the initial stage it could be closed due to sheer lack of use, or movement, beyond its small, everyday-speaking range. Panditji would say that the more the voice was exercised and nourished in the lower notes, the more it would open out naturally in the higher notes. Next, he would emphasise that all singing be in the "haa-kaar", (singing haa-wise, or from the navel), and not "aa-wise", or from the throat. Unique to this style was the cultivation of an "indrawn" voice throw, the pressure or force of the voice directed inward during singing, towards the source rather than otherwise. This facilitated a "de-materialisation" of the external voice, and a discovery of the voice's own abstract character, shorn of sensuality and external glamour. For the abstract was the real inner voice, the key to the mystic.

Training involved release of the "false" conditioning at the mental level, for the mind alone harboured obstructions and the mind alone could release them as well. Here, the guru's music acted as the mirror in which students could see for themselves what disturbed the purity of their own flow. As each day brought the scum to the surface, they would shed it, once they saw it. That was the methodology for "realisation" through naada sadhana.

As the student released blockages from his psyche, he,

simultaneously, released them from his prana or lifeforce as well, blockages that had disturbed the free flow of naada or cosmic energy through him. This gave him a tremendous sense of liberation and spiritual freedom; a renewed sense of life.

After years of practice and correction of the psyche, the voice, turned inward, began to open its "jawari", or a kind of mystic resonance not only of the soul having touched its Source, but the Source too, unveiling Itself, having actively illumined it.

This teaching had a special appeal not only for students of music but also of theatre, i.e., students of the voice, especially abstract theatre. Over the years, Panditji also taught the disciples of Grotowski, pioneer of the abstract theatre movement in Europe, who, in turn, had discovered in the special voice culture of the Indore style a methodology that not only helped unveil the "inner" voice but one that also offered another definition of immortality.

Make Music in Tempest and in Quietude

By Janina Gomes

USIC is born on two occasions: in times of tempest and storm and in times of rest. In times of tempest, music is brought out of us. In times of rest, we catch up with the melody of life. If we go flitting from one activity to another, from one place to another, we could end up with void.

Mrs Charles Cowman tells of the legend of a German baron who, at his castle on the Rhine, stretched wires from tower to tower, that the winds may convert them into an Aeolian harp. The soft breezes played about the castle, but no music was born.

One night there arose a great tempest. The hills and castle were assaulted by the fury of the mighty winds. The baron went to the threshold to look out upon the terror of the storm. He found the Aeolian harp was filling the air with strains that rang out above the clamour of the tempest. The tempest was needed to bring out the music.

When we are in a period of calm prosperity, we may not be able to produce any wonderful music. The tempest drives people to tune their Aeolian harps and to produce music with their lives.

The second occasion when we are most prone to produce music is during a period of rest, when our lives seem to produce nothing. But it is in times of rest that we create new melodies and hear new songs.

It is during the desert periods of our life that we begin to really listen to the call and voice of God that is sometimes most audible in silence.

Both periods can be of great darkness. Tempestuous times may find us buffeted by the strong storms of life. If we are out at sea and not in harbour, we may find it difficult to draw into a sheltered place safe from the storm. Life tosses us around and we may find it difficult to navigate rough waters even if we are guided by a compass.

But, it is in the very process of groping around and fighting the tempest that we find we have inner strength and derive a strong sense of purpose. Our own Aeolian harps get tuned to play music that makes the world richer for its sounds.

It is not age alone that improves the quality of the fibre of wood in a ship, but the straining and wrenching of the vessels by the sea, the chemical action of the bilge water and of the many kinds of cargoes it carries. It is the same with human lives stressed and tested in times of conflict and strife.

In times of rest, however, it may seem as though we are doing nothing. Others judge us by our actions. We act and react and as long as we are in the race, people rarely stop to question us because they so rarely question themselves. But in times of silence and rest, we hear the deeper sounds of creation and of the soul. We catch up with the harmonies and melodies of creation.

Mrs Cowman says that the polyps which construct the coral reefs, work away silently under water, never dreaming that they are building the foundation of a new island on which, by and by, life emerges. During periods of rest, motion is at an unseen level. In times of rest we grow, we connect more deeply with nature, with the universe and all life. We have to learn in times of tempest to ride the storm and in times of rest to create new horizons.

Salve For the Soul in Sound of Music

By Mrinalini Sarabhai

SOUND leads to understanding unity and divinity. Hence, the importance given to recitation of the sacred syllable "Om". The Sangeetanataka says that consciousness of Nada Brahmn leads to enlightenment. Rishi Matanga in Brhaddesi says: "Without nada neither song nor dance can exist—the entire universe is the embodiment of nada."

The songs of Samaveda are precursor of all Indian music. The singers of these chants participated in all sacred ceremonies. Positive sound is productive; it creates greater understanding and unity and is closest to the divine. Depictions of gods and goddesses in India reflect the importance of music in spiritual evolution—Nataraja dancing with the damraku; Krishna with the eternal flute; Saraswati, goddess of learning, with her veena; Nandi and his maddalam; Narada, the singer, wandering the earth, tanpura in hand. Music is an intrinsic part of Indian spirituality. When Maitreyi asked her husband, Sage Yagnavalkya, why he was going away to the forest, he replied, "When the veena is played one does not try to grasp the sound that is being played, one seeks the player of the veena. When the drum is played one does not grasp the drumming, one seeks the drummer. It is that limitless Self of our creation, the Atman, that I seek."

The notes of music have symbolic meaning; they evoke varied moods. Sa and Ri are to be used for rasas of vira or heroism, adbhuta or wonder and rudra or anger. Dha denotes bibhatsa or revulsion and bhaya or fear. Ga and Ni project karuna or compassion and Ma and Pa, hasya rasa or humour and sringara or the erotic. Each note activates and affects different cells of body and mind. Most temples of South India have mani mantapas with stone pillars that play music when struck with a thin stick and emit different notes of the musical scale. The legendary musician, Tansen, reportedly brought rain to the parched earth by singing raga Malhar. In the south, Viraraghava Iyer sang raga Vasanta to allay the heat and was known as Tsallagali (cool breeze) Iyer ever since. South India's Thyagaraja reportedly brought to life a person presumed dead, with raga Bihari. That's why many believe in the miraculous healing powers of music.

The Sufi poet, Hafiz, tells us of how God made a model of a clay figure and requested the human soul to enter within. But the soul refused to be imprisoned. However, when God asked the angels to play beautiful music, the soul made its entry. Hippocrates, the Greek who pioneered the western system of medicine, used music in the healing process. Today, it is proven that when used selectively, music can indeed heal. The term, "Mozart effect", has evolved from the fact that the composer's music has helped strengthen the mind, reduce tension, enhance creativity and heal the body of those who turned to it for succour. Japa or chanting of mantras has been a traditional daily ritual in India. It helps us connect to the source of all creation and the resonance of the last syllable of Om is a healing sound.

Whatever the music, if it is spiritually moving, it elevates the spirit and affects positively both mind and body. While good music is highly beneficial, today's cacophony of loud noises in the environment aggravates stress and will eventually destroy us. Loudspeakers used during festivals and other public functions and constant noise generated by traffic are all serious health hazards. Remember, sound is a powerful force—it can heal but it can also destroy.

Sangeet Marga: Path to Moksha

By V K Rangra

CCORDING to the Hindu view of creation, it was sound and not light that appeared first. In Vedic parlance, it is called Nada Brahmn or the Sound Celestial. Vedic rishis believed that the evolution of the Brahmand or universe was caused as a result of Bindu Visphot or an atomic explosion that produced infinite waves of sound, which represent cosmic ascent and expansion. The sound was the monosyllable: Om. Since Om is related to the beginning of the universe, Hindus consider it the most sacred syllable with which Vedic mantras commence.

Om is the principal name of the Supreme Being. It refers to all that is manifest and beyond. This is evident in Bhagavad Gita where Lord Krishna says: "I am the syllable Om in all the veda and sound in ether." According to Vedic literature, music originated from nada or sound, which is the product of akash or ether. There are two types of sound. The ahat or struck sound is audible, whereas the anahata or unstruck sound is inaudible. Sound originates in living beings from the friction between air, pran vayu or vital breath, and agni or heat energy (will power). It evolves first in a causal form as anahata and then in a gross form, ahat. When the gross form of sound emanates from the vocal chord and is sweet and soothing, it is called sangeetam or music. The anahata nada is most significant for yogis who have reached the highest level of consciousness. It is the internal sound they hear, after prolonged meditation and arduous yogic discipline. Ordinary human beings are engaged with the ahat nada.

Indian musical traditions trace the origin of music to Sama Veda. It is a compendium of melodies, chants and rules required for the recitation of sacred hymns. It serves as a textbook for priests officiating at Soma sacrifices. Lord Krishna in the Gita identifies himself with Sama Veda: "Of all the Vedas, I am the Sama Veda." Vedic chants are set in a musical pattern, collectively known as Samgan. To this day, the chants are in three accented musical patterns called swaras, precursor of the present seven-note musical system. Indra's musicians in Swargalok excelled in various forms of this art. The apsaras were the dancers; kinnaras were instrumentalists and gandharvas, celestial singers.

In Hindu mythology, each god is associated and identified with a particular musical instrument or some aspect of music. For example: Shiva: damru, Vishnu: shankh, Saraswati: veena, Ganesha: mridang, Krishna: flute and Narad: ektara. Shiva is believed to be the originator of five principal ragas: Bhairav,

Shri, Vasant, Pancham and Megh. Parvati, his consort, contributed the sixth, Natnarayana.

Music came to be divided into two categories: Marga or Vedic sangeet, the sacred music which pleased the gods, and Desi or Laukik, the profane or popular music serving human beings. Marga sangeet was created by the gods. It liberates the soul.

Natya Shastra, the first comprehensive treatise on Indian musical arts, is considered to be the fifth Veda. According to Bharata, its author, the gods, urged Brahma to compose a new Veda which would contain teachings of all the scriptures. So Brahma, taking the recitation from Rig Veda, songs from Sama Veda, histrionic representation from Yajur Veda and sentiments from Atharva Veda, created the new Veda. Brahma taught this Veda to Bharata, who, in turn, instructed his hundred sons who became authorities on music, dance and drama. Sage Yajnavalkya in his smriti shows the way to liberation: "The person well-versed in veena vadana and possessing deep knowledge of shruti, jati and tala of music, very easily obtains moksha."

Singing For the Grace of God

By Shammi Paranjape

HERE is a Sufi story that says how God made a statue out of clay in his own image. He asked the soul to enter into this image. But the soul did not like the idea of getting captive in this form and preferred to be free. God then asked the angels to play music and as they did, the soul was so moved to ecstasy that it willingly entered the body in order to fully experience the music. The story illustrates the power that music has, it can enthral us and hold us in its grip.

Our life starts and is sustained by the rhythmic murmur of our heartbeats, and it is no wonder then, that rhythm and beat should affect us so profoundly. The musical rendition of anything delights the heart. Even God, our scriptures declare, loves devotional songs or keertanam and rushes to any place where devotees gather to sing His glory. He is gaana vilola and bhava priya, lover of song and lover of feeling... The divine sage, Narada, expounded to humanity how singing His name joyously pleased God immensely and attracted His grace. Music is a remarkable bridge between the world of matter and the world of spirit. Saints recognised this mystic connection and used music to attune themselves to God.

Singing or chanting the glory of the divine is a tradition in most religions. We have Christmas carols and psalms, Buddhist and Jewish chants and chanting of the Qur'an. In the Hindu religious tradition, music has played an important role in the lives of people since the time of Sama Veda. Sri Sathya Sai Baba says that the three essential components of music—bh-bhav, ra-raga and ta-taal—when joined together give us "Bharat".

Devotional singing is an integral part of our ceremonies as also our worship and adoration of God. It is recognised as one of the nine modes of nav-vidha bhakti for attaining God's grace. It is one of the easiest paths to liberation, especially in this Kaliyug. In keertanam, we do not just take the name of God, we sing it... The advantage of singing the name over plain recitation is the ananda it confers on the singer and the listener alike. Sacred vibrations are produced which create a thrilling atmosphere surcharged with love. The weariness of samsar falls away and the singers feel attuned to their higher selves.

Down the ages, many saints have glorified the tradition of singing God's name. They recognised the power of keertanam to stir the depths of the human soul and exhorted weary humanity to avail of this simple road to bliss. The sixteenth century saint Chaitanya Mahaprabhu was one of the foremost exponents of this joyous celebration of God's love in ecstatic song. He spent his life in popularising this mode of devotion amongst the people. Saint Mirabai attained an exalted state of mind singing soulfully to her beloved Giridhar Gopal or Lord Krishna. To this day, Mira bhajans hold our spiritual imagination and cast a spell on the listener. In the devotional tradition of India, keertanam in its pure technical form comprises compositions of great devotees that were sung by trained artistes with musical accompaniments. However, for lay people there are other popular forms of devotional singing like bhajan or sankeertan sung in groups with simple tunes easily followed by all. Here, raga or melody and taal or rhythm become subservient to bhav or feeling as inspired devotees give collective voice to their deep aspirations for God. This group singing, which comprises mainly recitals of the divine names or a description of the attributes and leelas of the Lord, creates a powerful vibration, filling the heart with divine energy.

Guru Nanak popularised congregational singing with the aim of promoting the unity and spiritual welfare of the people. Musical instruments like mridang, chaplis and manjiras are used by devotees. Apart from the individual benefit, bhajan purifies the atmosphere by its positive vibrations. The idea behind devotional singing is to drop all self-consciousness and give oneself over completely to the joy of singing to the Lord. Only then does the energy created by the spirited keertan powerfully envelop all in a kind of transcendental rapture... Sant Jnaneshwar summed it beautifully, "By the power of chanting the Lord's name collectively, vaikuntha or heaven comes down into the mortal world for all..."

Shabad-Kirtan: The Highway of Bliss

By Kulbir Kaur

UCH is the extent of importance attached to the life of a householder that the sight of a sannyasi Sikh, who has renounced family life in pursuit of personal salvation, is a rare phenomenon. Even meditation, a way to salvation, is not an individual act in Sikhism, but rather Shabad-Kirtan performed in sangat is prescribed as the most influential means to attain the spiritual heights of meditation.

Guru Arjan, the fifth Guru, said, "Individual recitation of the Word is like water supply from a well which can irrigate the field of one person, whereas kirtan is like a cloudburst which turns the crops green in many fields." Shabad-Kirtan, singing of the glories of God with devotion, is considered not only as the most effective but also the easiest way to realise God in Sikhism. The word "Shabad" refers to the holy name or "Nam". Kirtan, a part of devotional worship, means singing praises of God. Shabad-Kirtan occupies a central place in all Sikh rites and ceremonies.

The tradition of Shabad-Kirtan was started by Guru Nanak who believed "the disciples when engrossed in singing of the glories of God, realise their own identity with the Lord". This tradition was greatly influenced by the devotional form of worship of the Bhakti movement. The bhaktas were not only great saints but also musicians and made Indian sacred music richer with their compositions of outstanding merit. Guru Nanak also spread his message fusing it with sweet melodies of music. No wonder, the hymns in Guru Granth Sahib are all arranged by music, based on thirty-one ragas.

Out of 1,430 pages of the Adi Granth, 1,343 are set in various musical tunes. In course of time, the Sikh devotional music came to be known as "Shabad-Kirtan" and the tradition of singing the holy hymns to the accompaniment of instruments continues till today.

Shabad-Kirtan in congregation may be performed in a gurdwara, in a private residence or in any other place. The sangat may chant the sacred hymns in unison, or a group of musicians, known as Raagis, may perform Kirtan as is often the case. Those, who for some reason, cannot do Kirtan, should listen to the Kirtan and join in the chorus which produces the same enchanting feeling, inspiring the human soul towards spiritual reality.

The realisation of the vision of God can be attained by connecting the level of consciousness, at the time of Shabad-Kirtan, with the meaning of hymns and understanding their true message. The Guru says, "As all humans have the divine spark in them, by singing or listening to sacred music, their hearts are inclined to concentrate on the Almighty, who in turn may lead them to a spiritual vision." Shabad-Kirtan, or the chanting of the holy word, links one's heart to God and also calms the mind by making it contented. "Singing, listening to Kirtan with devotion in mind removes sorrow and brings lots of happiness to man." The Guru says it removes jealousy from the mind and also imparts the values of seva or service and namrata or humility among listeners.

"By singing the praises of God, the dirt is washed away, and the evil of ego is removed." Shabad-Kirtan is not only a means of religious, ethical and moral training, but congregational singing in praise of God also binds people into a social unit inculcating among listeners values of brotherhood, equality and seva, sidelining all considerations of caste, religion, gender or social status. This way of meditation for salvation is regarded as the simplest to perform, due to lack of any rituals or need for elaborate arrangements. Shabad-Kirtan is divine music, "an invaluable diamond, full of bliss and profound qualities".

Music Dissolves All Divisions

By Lama Doboom Tulku

S I looked into my calendar for the year, I found I was visiting so many countries to attend festivals of sacred music. I looked back. What began in Tibet House as an idea of spreading the message of peace and harmony through music, slowly grew into a string of five festivals to be held in five different continents. In no time the idea assumed proportions larger than that which could be contained in five festivals. Within a year, since the main global event was held in Bangalore, we have celebrated some ten festivals in different countries. The snowballing effect of the idea goes on unabated and festivals have been planned in Japan, Australia and other parts of the world.

Music, in general, and sacred music, in particular, has the quality of creating an atmosphere of peace and harmony. Even wild animals, it is said, stop hunting when they hear music. It is not only that listening to music can make your mind more tranquil, but also when we think of music, generally, it is not within a narrow kind of identity, community-related or nationality. At that moment, the mind transcends all boundaries. At that moment, there is no religion. The festival at Bangalore, for example, found Islamic singers from Indonesia, rendering the Gayatri Mantra.

In all festivals, when musicians interacted, neither language, caste nor community came between them. They looked for synthesis and combinations, with harmony as their overriding concern. The root of the trouble then is division; division between you and others. And music does not recognise this division. It brings people together. That is why we have music associated with various aspects of life and spiritual progress too. It is said in Bodhicharyavatra of Santideva: "Athaha param pratishttatham pujamegha manoramaha, turya sangeeta meghascha sarva satva prahashnnaha." That is to say, in addition to all other offerings to the Buddha and the Boddhisattvas, may a host of offerings, resounding with lilting music, sweet and resounding to the ears of all beings, be also offered for it eases the suffering of sentient beings. As a finale to elaborate ritual worship, Santideva adds the sound of sangita, devotional music accompanied with song and dance, and the playing of such instruments as muraja and turya.

The second reason for the success of the idea of a festival of sacred music was the association of His Holiness the Dalai Lama, known all over the world as a symbol of peace and harmony. Although His Holiness is a leader of the Tibetan people, when he travels around the world, he has been speaking mostly about uplift of basic human values. Music was a good way of spreading His Holiness's concerns. It also came at a time when people were excited about the coming in of the new millennium, the new century. People were and are, at this point in time, looking for a better future, a better world.

How can the future turn brighter or the world turn better? Only by fostering basic human values. It is this desire within man that has made music festivals popular. The intention was to plant seeds of peace and harmony in the minds of the people, especially the younger generation. This is important because the human race is facing the danger of losing some of its basic human qualities of compassion, wisdom and potential for spiritual growth.

All traditional values may not be relevant today, but some of them are of great importance at all times. One among them is the desire and value placed on mental peace. Mental peace, not in terms of just tranquillity but a little more, a deep-rooted understanding and appreciation of basic human qualities.

As told to Sudhamahi Regunathan

Spirituality, the Soul of Our Music

By Sumitra Guha

HIS story goes back to the days of Akbar. Mighty pleased with the music of Tansen, the Mughal emperor thought to himself: "If the maestro is so mellifluous, what would the music of his guru be like?" Resolved to hear the master who had honed the gem of his darbar, Akbar donned a disguise and reached the dilapidated temple which was the abode of Swami Haridas. And when the guru sang a paean to his Lord, Akbar stood mesmerised. "How come your music does not work in this same way, Tansen?" the emperor asked his navaratna. "Simple," explained the Mian of Malhar. "I sing for the emperor, but my guru sings for the emperor of emperors." In that sentence Mian Tansen encapsulated the essence of Indian classical music.

Beyond doubt, the most important quality of our music is its spirituality. It is not a coincidence, since our music started with recitation of shlokas by the Vedic sages. We know for sure that the entire Sama Veda was transmitted through melody. The sages recognised the musical quality of natural sounds, and all the seven notes of the Sargam are named after the bull, the frog, the koel... In fact, clusters of these sounds such as Jhim, Hrim were used for meditation. Sample Dhrupad and you'll know the truth of the contention.

The music of Carnatic saints too is a standing example of the point that Indian music is basically spiritual. Beginning with Annamacharya, the southern saints have proved that you can realise God through music. While the singer attains bliss through singing, listeners experience the same bliss by sharing the music. Annamacharya stated this through a symbolic act. The saint had written 34,000 compositions, in a language that was a mix of Telugu and Sanskrit. Only one of these he laid at the feet of Venkateswara and said, "If people realise the import of this song, they will see the Lord through my eyes."

Why talk of the south alone? The same sentiment is echoed when Ramakrishna Paramhansa says, "You too can see the goddess as plainly as I do. Only, you too must pray to her with your entire being." Purandara Dasa, Meera Bai, Surdas, Kabir—they all chose music to arrive at their goal. If their ditties reverberate through the length and breadth of the land, span centuries, and live in the heart of millions, it only shows that Nadopasana (worship through music) is as powerful a mode of attaining god as Gyan Marg.

When did this kinship wear off? Why do we find beat nudging out the meditative quality of Indian music? The onset can be traced to the days when invaders were destroying much of the art that was an expression of our religion. And when Indian music moved from the temple to the court, its spiritual quality had to give way to its sensual beauty. This was stressed since music, like dance, was now for entertainment alone. Soon, music was left to flourish in the kothas, and that drove the nail into the mystic quality of raga music. Today, instead of synchronising with all the other elements of music, beat dominates all else, including lyrics which pave the way to a listener's heart. But in the long run, fast tempo, particularly at the cost of melody, will increase the stress level and with it the incidence of heart ailment.

A Yugoslavian settled in France, Milovan Stankov, visits the Himalayas every summer. Every year he also hosts in Paris a festival of Indian devotional music. In his own words, "the peace I get in your music is matched only by the peace in your philosophy." I am convinced that, sooner rather than later, people will realise the spiritual strength of Indian music. I have seen it at my concerts in Paris, Zurich, New York... People passing by have walked in, stayed on, and come backstage with tears in their eyes.

A mother heard Yashoda's entreaty to Balgopal—Abto ghar aaja—and set out in quest of her estranged teenager son. An estranged couple regained harmony on hearing a Maru Bihag exposition on its need in the short journey that is our lives. None of them was deterred by the language of the bhajan. An explanation in English, coupled with the melody, is enough to unveil to them the rasa—be it Bhakti, Vatsalya or Shringar—which is the mainstay of our musical compositions. All that is required to rejuvenate this quality is to rekindle the spirituality within us. For, it is only through the voice of the singer that the depth of feeling reaches out to the listener and provides him a tantalising glimpse of the all-pervading Almighty.

Moving Monsoon Ragas Help Unite Self With Nature

By Himani Dalmia

NDIAN classical art forms express the artiste's subjective, internal experience. The human is invariably viewed as part of nature. In paintings, humans are accorded the same space as a flower or a creeper. Art relates the inner to the outer, the material to the spiritual.

The system of ragas in classical music centres on the expression of a core feeling, a "rasa". The note-by-note expansion or vistaar of the raga allows emotion to be articulated wholly, each note adding a new dimension to the mood already created by the musician. This teasing out of the raga parallels the development of the musician's feeling, until both the raga and emotion blossom fully.

This relationship can perhaps be understood best when we consider monsoon ragas. The monsoon season is rich in emotional diversity and Malhar ragas help nature, emotion and art to converge. Trees become green and heavy with fruit, the mating season begins and the sound of thunder rents the air. The ambience is one of romance and joy. At the same time, dark and brooding clouds invoke a sense of fear. Mythology speaks of monsoon rainstorms, complete with menacing bolts of lightning as expressions of Indra's wrath. Ragamala paintings depicting raga Megh show Krishna dancing with gopis in ecstasy; he also holds up the Govardhan mountain to shelter his people from Indra's outpouring.

The compositions in Malhar ragas are inspired by the personality of rain. The shudh or natural and komal or flattened "Ni" note intertwines in these ragas to evoke running water. A certain fluidity is also suggested through "meends", the smooth transition from one note to another. The fast "taans" recall the sound of falling rain. The Malhar ragas can be both cheerful and sombre. Raga Megh creates a significantly brighter mood than the darker Miya ki Malhar, allowing the musician to relate to all aspects of this season.

A common theme in monsoon ragas is that of pining for one's lover. The compositions often speak of the anticipation felt by the beloved for the company of her lover, seeking his protection from the thunderstorm. Several Ragamala paintings depict a woman rushing indoors to her lover against a backdrop of dark clouds, rain and lightning. The dominant mood is of longing after separation, the monsoon complementing the turbulence in minds of anxious lovers.

Kalidasa's classic work, Meghadoota, the Cloud Messenger, uses the monsoon as a metaphor to convey yearning and love. The poem blends man and nature, as the cloud and lover become inseparable symbols of that core feeling: longing.

It is no coincidence that artistes over the ages have sought to translate the essence of monsoons into tangible art, whether in Ragamala paintings, poetry or Malhar ragas. The rendering of a monsoon raga is a dialogue between the rasa and the artiste, and a fusion of the individual and nature. The people of the subcontinent sense that monsoons somehow serve to connect us with something larger than the self. This longing for a connection—with a lover, with nature, or even with God—is the essence and spirit of monsoon ragas.

Sweeping Wisdom From a Youth in Haridwar

By Seema Burman

E spent a tension-filled week in the office recently with many of us awaiting news of promotions and increments. As rumours snowballed, hurried meetings took place in corridors. Some people were ashen-faced, others were jumping with joy. Some criticised the "system", others consulted experts. I decided to escape to Haridwar and experience a peaceful meditative week.

The ashram was serene and peaceful. All one could hear was the chirping of birds. In the afternoon, a smiling boy of 25 came to clean our room. He said he could not come earlier as he had to clean 50 rooms all on his own. Seeing my shocked expression, the boy grinned and assured me that it wasn't that bad a situation. He revealed that he had joined just three days ago as a sweeper-cleaner. A month back, he was working as a motor mechanic in a private company but got laid off with many others. Wasn't that terrible, I inquired gently. "No, Ma'am. It's all destined. I am young and hard working and I will find a good job again, God willing. Why should I worry?" But a loss of Rs 5,000 wasn't small, I pursued. "Money comes and goes, like this Ma'am", he said and snapped his fingers. What a brave boy, I thought. And here was I who had "escaped" to the serenity of Haridwar. Despite a string of academic degrees, achievements and experience we still panic because we are afraid we would not move to the next grade.

Life is in itself a laboratory that helps us observe and learn if only we keep our eyes and ears open. No wonder a ripe mind like Dattatreya's could learn from nature and make not one or two but 24 gurus from his wanderings. These were: earth, air, sky, water, fire, moon, sun, pigeon, python, ocean, archer, moth, snake, bee, spider, firefly, fish, deer, hawk, honey-gatherer, child, elephant, sparrow and a courtesan, Pingala.

To learn from life and one's experiences, one must be open, receptive and flexible. Learning is a state of consciousness that enables one to learn from all situations if only one retains the innocence of a child. Even a humble servant can teach us qualities of generosity, forgiveness, unselfishness and the strength to bear burdens.

Swami Chinmayananda said that the road sign "U Turn" could be taken as an indicator that we ought to turn the direction of our life towards spirituality instead of trying to change others. Ordinarily, when we listen to saints, read scriptures and attend satsangs, we examine and dissect the speech and actions of the saint, even if he is one's guru. Thus, we shift from guru to guru, looking through the prism of ego. We are unable to understand the essence of teachings because we fail to become a disciple. So, even when Krishna Himself asks us to accept success and failure with equanimity once our job is done, we still get extremely miserable at failures and are elated at success.

To understand wisdom, you need not listen to moralistic lectures, or intellectual sermons. All you need is a childlike mind, a mind free of concepts and rigid ideas. With such a flexible mentality, wisdom flows from every side; from road signs, servants, spiders, snakes, courtesans and children. Then, all of existence becomes your guru because you are a disciple. You would be able to face all kinds of situations and there would be no reason to run to sages for practical advice on how to manage your daily life.

Mathematical Equation For Eternal Happiness

By K S Iyer

THE definition of happiness varies from person to person. It varies even from one stage of life to another. Is it possible to arrive at a formula that conforms to everyone's definition of happiness? M K Gandhi found an answer to this question in the first verse of Isha Upanishad that said: "Renounce and enjoy." This was his reply to a western journalist who challenged him to reveal the secret of his happiness in just three words.

When we express this secret in mathematical terms, the connection between renunciation and happiness becomes clear: $H=R/N$—where H stands for happiness/contentment, R for resources at your command and N for your needs. As the quantum of your needs starts decreasing, the "H" quotient keeps increasing. If you can bring down the "N" factor to zero, "H" reaches infinity. Such a feat is almost impossible for the average person. Also, there is a danger of misinterpreting the concept of renunciation. It is not the gloominess of self-denial but the extinguishing of the candle because dawn has arrived. It is a highly evolved mind that understands that it is better to need less than to want and have more.

Most live out their lives assuming that existing resources are insufficient to fulfil their needs. This economic thought process leads to "scarcity" and so there arises conflict, each individual or a group fighting for himself or itself.

Isha Upanishad invocation contradicts all that. Social Darwinism is based on the economics of materialism. But spiritual economics begins not from the assumed scarcity of matter but from the verifiable infinity of contentment.

This argument sounds logical and convincing, but how practical is it? We live in a flat world where other people's affluence sets standards for us. We need to break the mould of consumerist thinking. That the materialistic West is increasingly turning to the spiritual East for inspiration is an eye-opener. When Gandhi used ahimsa or non-violence to overcome the British dominion, the idea was dismissed by many as being impractical. But ahimsa did win.

In our pursuit of happiness, we must be wrong somewhere for happiness seems to have become a rare commodity. Those seeking happiness through material acquisitions find their quest is futile. Even though we tire ourselves in search of happiness, it is doubtful if we would recognise it if we did find it. Do we really know what makes us happy? A successful person by society's standards is not necessarily a happy person. Because happiness has nothing to do with possessions, environment or even physical health. Happiness comes from a source that is independent of all these. Genuine happiness is a state of contentment that comes with peace of mind and a sense of well-being regardless of outward circumstances.

You will find happiness when you stop comparing your life and possessions with other people's. There will always be bigger houses, better and more expensive than the one you have. Accept the fact that there are some things in life that you can't change. God's blessings come to us in three forms—pleasure, joy and happiness. Pleasure comes from satisfying our physical senses, joy comes from association with others but happiness results from a fulfilling relationship with God. Everything comes from God and returns to God. And God has provided enough for everyone's need but not for everyone's greed.

Why Krishna Watched As Gopis Lifted Water

By Shammi Paranjape

ONCE the gopikas of Vrindavan were lifting heavy pails of water, while their cowherd friend, Krishna, stood by and watched. He made no move to help them. The gopis marked His strange indifference. However, a little later when they wanted to remove the pails from their heads and place them on the ground, Krishna rushed to help them. Asked why, He replied that His task was to help human souls unburden themselves, not assist them in adding burdens.

Often, we pray for the very things that God does not want to give us: added burdens. We seek fame, fortune and power but none of these give us the happiness we are seeking. Why? Simply because all these are external and related to the world whereas true happiness is internal and related to the spirit. We may strew our lives with pleasures, but that will not help because there is a vast difference between pleasure and happiness. The former is related to the senses and is evanescent; the latter is of and from the soul and is abiding.

How to attain soul-abiding happiness? The scriptures have a stunning thing to say... they tell us that there is nothing to attain for we are sat-chitananda or embodiments of bliss, it is just a question of realising it. The whole aim of life is this self-realisation. To reach this, one has to turn one's gaze and attention inward, away from the material world, to the inner essence of being.

"Whether one is a yogi or a bhogi; whether one is a sanyasi or householder, he alone will be truly happy and will verily enjoy, who is ever revealing inwardly in Brahmn," said Adi Sankara in Bhaja Govindam.

It is maya or illusion that creates the universe and spreads before the mind the vast paraphernalia of the objective world. It is a nartaki or enchantress who entices the intelligence and traps the senses. Every material thing is a decoy to make you lose your way to the spirit. It's like chasing mirages one after another.

The more you clear the clutter of worldly desires and negative thoughts, the more space is created for the spirit to surface and roam free. Desire in itself is not a bad thing; it is limitless desire that creates havoc and destroys peace.

A basic concept underlying the Hindu attitude to life is that of the four ends of man or purusharthas: dharma, righteousness; artha, wealth; kama, desire; and moksha, liberation. An emancipated and integrated approach to human experience is reflected in the four purusharthas. Dharma is the regulating factor and if artha and kama are kept within the parameters of dharma, the individual will, in the natural course, proceed towards the final and supreme aspiration, moksha.

Since material pleasures can never provide complete fulfilment, it is worthwhile to enquire deeply where true satisfaction and happiness lie. For this, one has to awaken the spiritual senses which exist in a dimension different to that of our limited physical senses.

Sathya Sai Baba says: "Less luggage, more comfort, make travel a pleasure. On this journey of life our desires are our baggage. The fewer our desires the greater our comfort... many people interpret renunciation to mean either giving away as charity, money or land or donning the ochre robe; but real renunciation is the giving up of desire."

Why Children Smile a Lot and Adults Are Grouchy

By H S Gopalan

APPINESS is a state of mind. External factors like wealth, money, and comforts they bring by themselves cannot make you happy. Buddha said all earthly possessions and trappings are bondages which bring miseries.

Happiness is a state brought about by your being satisfied with what you have got. Be mentally prepared for whatever befalls you. It is only when you develop a sense of not being satisfied with what you have got and crave for more and more that happiness drifts away and unhappiness sets in.

We smile when something pleasant or pleasurable happens. A smile is an involuntary reflection of happiness. Many simple and small things which cost us nothing make us smile. Meeting a beloved, friend or relative, seeing the sun breaking through the clouds after a dark rainy day, a rainbow, a sudden gentle breeze on a hot afternoon, all these things make us happy and light up our faces.

Look at a newborn. Within a few days, she starts smiling on seeing a recognisable face. What makes her smile? The child smiles and laughs on seeing a toy or the moon. It is her reaction to being pleased and satisfied. A child smiles 400 to 500 times a day and when we grow into adults, the number of smiles per day comes down drastically. A child does not have much expectation. She is happy because she is pleased with whatever she gets. One could always be like a child—in a state of happiness by being satisfied and contented. Though difficult to achieve, it is not impossible.

Happiness can also be achieved by realising that things could have been worse. But it is not in this negative sense alone that one can be happy. Whenever we are unhappy, we should try to recollect and remember how much happiness has come our way and the number of things we have, for which we should be thankful. We should count our blessings and look at the silver lining in the clouds.

We blame God for whatever we are not blessed with, but do we thank God enough for everything he has blessed us with? Are we making the best use of whatever we have got?

There are innumerable things in life to be happy about. We are blessed with physical abilities, mental faculties, relatives, friends and with nature's bounties. The rest is what we make. Being contented does not imply that we should not be ambitious, but ambition should be within limits and should not turn into avarice.

You can have ambition to earn more money through legitimate means, so that you can not only improve your standard of living but also contribute generously to the community. But while doing so, one should not get so attached to material gains and comforts that even their temporary absence makes you feel miserable. The scriptures say we should be like a lotus in a pond which gets wet yet allows no drop of water to get stuck to it.

All religions talk of overcoming selfishness, to become selfless. Real happiness will come when one can get liberated to reach a state of nirvana. Nirvana is a state of perfect bliss, an ideal state where one reaches a transcendent consciousness in which there is neither suffering, desire nor sense of self and the subject is released from the effects of karma.

Achieve Eternal Premananda by Becoming a Gopi

By Parmarthi Raina

AN inspector-general of police in Lucknow recently dressed himself up as a gopi and danced about as one would in Krishna's rasa lila. People reacted with amusement, astonishment or shock. Some even declared the IGP crazy. To evolved Krishna devotees, however, it was very much a part of Vaishnava devotional tradition—Raganuga Bhakti Sadhana—that is practised by some sects in Vraja to this day.

Raganuga Bhakti Sadhana was first presented and elaborated by Srila Rupa Goswami, a disciple of Chaitanya Mahaprabhu, around five centuries ago in his treatise, Bhaktirasamrtasindhu or Ocean of the Nectar of Devotion. The sadhana is linked with drama and calls for the sadhaka or aspirant to act the part of a gopi in Krishna's rasa lila and, in so doing, transport himself physically, mentally and emotionally into the lila and experience the mood or bhava of the gopis. The sadhaka eventually begins to believe that he actually is a gopi and, thereby, attains premananda, or loving bliss, in the service of the Supreme Reality.

In the world of theatre, to attain perfection in the part they are playing, actors often adopt lifestyles of personalities they portray—to behave like them, to understand them, to think like them, to "become" them. Russian director and philosopher, Constantin Stanislavski, was among the first to propose to actors to "live your part". He discovered that dramatic acting could also change the life of an actor. While playing the role of Mahatma Gandhi, Ben Kingsley, for months, actually lived in Ahmedabad, emulating the austere and disciplined lifestyle of Mahatma Gandhi. Kingsley admitted that in playing the role, he even began to think like Gandhi and that it had an immense impact on his personal life. True actors become completely identified with the personality they are portraying. The result is complete fusion of the actor's life with the part he is playing, and there are moments when the actor finds it difficult to distinguish himself from the character he is portraying.

In pursuing Raganuga Bhakti Sadhana, the seeker, by continued emulation, gradually loses his social identity and accepts a new identity in the Spiritual or Ultimate Reality. During the transition, the individual lives and enacts both roles, one in the reality of everyday world and another in the make-believe spiritual world of Krishna's rasa lilas. Such was the case with the IG of police in Lucknow.

Raganuga Bhakti Sadhana is an aesthetic, religio-dramatic devotional practice that imitates the passion of the inhabitants of Vraja who love and adore their Krishna. It is an experience in bhakti rasa, whereby a bhakta can relish any one of the five main bhavas—shanta (neutral), dasya (servant), sakhya (friend), vatsalya (son or parent) and madhurya (sweet lover)—by emulating a character corresponding to that bhava. The most intimate and loving and, therefore, the most desired, is the madhurya bhava or the bhava that the gopis had for the bewitching cowherd, Krishna—the ultimate lover, the Ultimate Reality. To aid the enactment of a gopi's role to perfection, the actor must "live the role" and this necessitates him wearing the gopi's clothes and make-up, if necessary.

The Happiness Factor in Natural Evolution

By Anil K Rajvanshi

N a riverbed were two plants. One was the mighty banyan tree and the other was a reed. "You are spineless; look at me. Not only am I tall and stand erect, I also give shade to the weary," it would often say to the reed. In the rainy season came a flash flood that uprooted the banyan tree. The reed, however, survived as it simply bent with the current and when the floods receded it became erect again. This is a story of the strength of humility. Another great lesson the story contains is that it is only those systems that come in equilibrium with the surroundings that survive.

Evolution of natural systems normally takes place via branching when the system goes far from equilibrium or "becomes unwieldy", and is governed by laws of non-linear thermodynamics. The branch which comes into equilibrium with the surrounding forces survives and prospers.

Coming into equilibrium with surroundings also means actively interacting with surrounding forces like sun, wind, atmosphere and gravity. A system can only interact with the surrounding forces when it can sense them. Thus, natural systems have developed mechanisms for sensing all these elements and, hence, have temperature, humidity, solar, chemical and gravity sensors.

Most times we are unhappy because of conflict within the self or with the surroundings. To resolve the conflict or come "in equilibrium" we should be able to sense our surroundings. The first mechanism for happiness is, therefore, to become acutely aware of the surroundings and corresponding forces. This means developing a sensitive mind and increasing one's awareness. Both these are produced by making our minds powerful through Yoga. A powerful mind is a great information processor and, hence, can process signals and information from the surroundings very efficiently. Without awareness, the interaction with the forces is only a one-way affair, that is, we are controlled by them.

This enhanced awareness also helps us to become non-violent towards nature and our fellow human beings because we can start understanding the other person's point of view. Similarly, it also gives us strength to make others aware of our point of view. This is the genesis of coming in equilibrium with the surroundings. If we approach a conflict, which could either be internal or external, in the spirit of compromise, then it has a mechanism to elicit a corresponding sentiment from the other person. This results in conflict resolution. Compromising, nevertheless, is not an easy process. It requires courage and quality thought to produce compromise formulas since a viable and an acceptable solution has to be provided. Gandhiji had made this compromise process into an art form and it was the reason for his success in finding solutions to difficult problems.

The ability to compromise is the second mechanism of happiness. Without compromise, the evolutionary path will be based on conflicts and may end in all-round destruction of both people and environment. Conflict resolution through mechanisms of awareness and compromise can produce true sustainability and happiness.

Transform Your Mind To Be Content and Happy

By Ramesh S Balsekar

IT is precisely the pursuit of happiness which prevents happiness from happening and, until this realisation happens, the pursuit must go on.

What is seeking happiness is Consciousness.

Impersonal consciousness had identified itself with a particular body-mind organism (form) and a name as a separate entity; and it is this trapped, unidentified consciousness which is seeking its personality. When the ego, the practical seeker of everything in life, takes over the search for happiness, pleasure is mistaken for happiness in the flow of life... The few egos that focus on real happiness become spiritual seekers, for they realise that what they are seeking is not to be found in the flow of life, but in their attitude.

The Greek word "metanoesis" implies changing the mind, but means transformation of mind. The Sanskrit word for it is "paravritti", meaning turning around at the deepest level of the heart-mind.

Paravritti tells the seeker-ego that happiness is one's natural state, hidden by hatred born of our perception of the "other" as a source of potential rivalry and enmity. We're instructed from childhood that life means competition with the other, and happiness means success over the other, in the classroom as well as playing fields. The other is seen as a potential enemy.

Whether or not we achieve happiness is based on our sense of personal doership. Buddha said, Events happen, deeds get done, consequences happen, but there is no individual doer of any deed. Everything in life is happening according to Cosmic Law.

What the sense of personal doership has done is that the human being, at any moment, is burdened with an enormous load of hatred for oneself for harming others, willingly or otherwise, and also for others who hurt us. The total acceptance of personal non-doership means the immediate removal of this load of hatred, and the absence of hatred automatically means the presence of our natural state: happiness, consisting of total peace and harmony.

The Sanskrit term "Sat-Chit-Ananda" means Existence-Consciousness-Ananda. Ananda is shanti or peace, not joy or ecstasy. The Buddha said that enlightenment means the end of suffering. Interestingly, the Buddha has used the negative perspective—end of suffering—rather than the positive one of joy or ecstasy. It is the experience of all of us, sometime or the other, that the sudden end of an intense pain has brought about an intensity of relief that was much more acceptable than any positive pleasure or joy. Pursuit of happiness is the very essence of living for all creatures on earth, beginning with the infant seeking its mother's breast. For the poor, happiness can only mean sufficient money to provide the minimum of food, clothing and shelter.

However, for those who are reasonably comfortable in life, it is the destiny of a few to look for happiness beyond what the flow of life could bring. In the case of the unselfish and generous, being generous gives them the happiness they seek, and not being generous would make them unhappy.

Ultimately, happiness means not something in the flow of life, it is the attitude to life. And the most important point about it is that there is no "doing" in it. It is a pure happening.

Love 24X7 Takes You To the State of Everlasting Joy

By Thich Nhat Hanh

FOUR important subjects are discussed in Samiddhi Sutra: the idea of happiness, the existence of real joy, the practice of reliance and the trap of complexes. Our notions about happiness entrap us. We forget that they are just ideas. Our idea of happiness can prevent us from actually being happy.

The second idea is that of the existence of real joy. When a goddess asked the young monk, Samiddhi, why he chose to abandon happiness in the present moment for a vague promise of happiness in the future, Samiddhi answered: "The opposite is true. It is the idea of happiness in the future that I have abandoned, so I can dwell deeply in the present moment."

The third topic the Sutra discusses is the practice of reliance or support. Relying on Dharma is not just an idea. When you live in accordance with the Dharma, you realise joy, tranquillity, stability and freedom. It is "taking refuge in the island of self", the island of peace in each of us. We must know how to return to that island when we need to. In his last moments, the Buddha said: "Take refuge in the island of self... There you will find Buddha, Dharma, and Sangha."

The fourth subject concerns the trap of complexes—thinking you are better than, worse than, or equal to others. The complexes arise because we think we are a separate self. Happiness built on the notion of a separate self is weak and unreliable. Through the practice of meditation, we come to see that we "inter-are" with all other beings and our fears, anxieties, anger and sorrow disappear. If you practise true happiness, relying on the Dharma and realising the interconnected and interdependent nature of all things, you become freer and more stable every day. Gradually, you will be in a paradise where the deep love described by the Buddha pervades.

Happiness is not an individual matter; it has the nature of interbeing. When you are able to make one friend smile, her happiness will also nourish you. When you find ways to peace, joy and happiness, you do it for everyone. Begin by nourishing yourself with joyful feelings. Practise walking, meditation outside, enjoying the fresh air, trees, stars in the night sky. What do you do to nourish yourself? It is important to discuss this subject with dear friends to find concrete ways to nourish joy and happiness.

When you succeed in doing this, your suffering, sorrow and painful mental formations will begin to transform. When your body is invaded by harmful bacteria, your antibodies surround the bacteria and render them harmless. When there aren't enough antibodies, your body will create more so it can neutralise the infection. Likewise, when you suffuse your body and mind with feelings of the joy of meditation, your body and spirit will be strengthened. Joyous feelings have a capacity to transform feelings of sorrow and pain in us.

The Buddha's teachings on love are clear. It is possible to live 24 hours a day in a state of love. The Four Immeasurable Minds are strong concentrations of love, compassion, joy and equanimity. When you dwell in these concentrations, you are living in the most beautiful, peaceful and joyous realm in the universe.

From the writer's *Teachings on Love*

Knowledge, Not Experience, Is Path To Anubhava

Satsang: Swami Dayananda

How can happiness be experienced?

WHENEVER you pick up a resolving moment of happiness, you experience your essential self. Through some gain, sensation, a profound appreciation of beauty, whatever, a certain mental condition occurs in which, for the moment, you are just with yourself. In the quiet clarity of a mind that wants no change whatsoever, you pick up a moment of ananda. You do not recognise that ananda as yourself; you attribute it to an object or a situation experienced.

Desiring ananda all the time, you continually seek it through all your actions. Nobody desires something that is unknown. You know what ananda is and that is why you want it. What you do not know is that you are ananda; you cannot help but seek it because it is your very nature and you cannot settle for anything else, for anything less. But you do know there is such a thing as ananda; that there are moments of fullness which are moments of happiness.

Even if you gain new experience which reveals ananda to you, it makes no difference. Whether the experiences you have are usual or unusual, they still have to be assimilated in terms of knowledge. Experience by itself does not give knowledge for experience. It comes and goes. Vedanta provides the basis for knowledge that the moment of happiness I experience reflects my real nature, ananda, limitlessness, fullness. Knowledge of the whole that frees me. For that knowledge, I need to know what is mithya, apparently real, and what is satyam, non-negatable reality. I have to account for this world or else things will not fall into place. Just slipping into myself is not enough. If I do not discover the nature of the world and that of myself, the world will overwhelm me and I will have to escape.

Vedanta has been erroneously presented as an experience. Vedanta is knowledge, not a happening; it is the immediacy of knowledge. When that immediacy of knowledge is presented as experience, confusion follows in part because the Sanskrit word, "anubhava," has been translated in English simply as "experience". This causes the expectation of a "happening", not a "seeing". "Anubhava" is immediate knowledge. That which is in keeping with the teaching is called anubhava. That which comes after the teaching is knowledge in keeping with the teaching. Experience is immediate knowledge.

Is happiness "realisation" rather than "experience"?

It is recognition in terms of knowledge. You recognise the truth of yourself in terms of knowledge—a knowledge that embraces you, your world, and God. In knowledge, you see the non-dual as a whole. Experience is only an escape from the perception of duality; knowledge accounts for duality. In knowledge, I face duality and see there is no duality. I appreciate and enjoy the world I perceive; at the same time I know there is no duality.

Knowledge requires a pramana, an instrument of knowledge and someone to wield that instrument. Shruti, scripture, is the pramana and the teacher wields the pramana, unfolding the words of Shruti until the student sees the fact of the whole and knows, "That whole I am."

Logical Deduction For Happiness In Life

By Ramesh Balsekar

AILY living has three aspects:
1) Each individual has a particular situation; this means deciding what you want in a given situation and doing whatever you think you should do to get it. Once you have done it, your free will has ended.

2) What happens after is not in your control. Experience shows that sometimes you have got what you wanted and sometimes you have not. Or what you have got has been totally unexpected, for better or worse.

3) Thereafter, society accepts what has actually happened as your own action, good or bad, and you are rewarded or punished.

Reward has come to mean pleasure and punishment has come to be understood as pain, all in the moment. We have no choice but to accept if we want to continue living in that society. This constitutes your happiness or unhappiness from moment to moment over which you have no control, nor can you know what will bring pleasure or pain, or know the total amount of pleasure and pain assigned to you during your lifetime. Happiness cannot depend on what you experience moment to moment. Therefore, happiness must depend upon your attitude to life.

It is important that you engage yourself in self-enquiry: what is your attitude to life that has prevented you from being happy? The main reason for our unhappiness is your relationship with the other. Daily living means your relationship with the other— whether the other is a close relative, a colleague at work or a total stranger.

You cannot be happy unless your relationship with the other is harmonious. Being happy is to be at peace with yourself, that is, never to be uncomfortable with yourself.

You are not totally comfortable with yourself in your relationship with the other because the other will not always do what you want him to do, and you cannot expect him to do that either! Does it mean that we can never be happy? That's not true because we know at least one or two people who enjoy the same pleasures we do, suffer the same pain, and yet they are transparently happy, never uncomfortable with themselves.

Another problem is apparently a dead end. The third force is the concept offered by the Buddha. You cannot expect the other always to do what you want him to do. No one really does anything. Events happen, deeds are done, consequences happen, but no one does any deed. Everything happens according to a Cosmic Law; how each happening affects whom in what way—for better or worse—is also according to Cosmic Law; therefore, no one can be blamed for any happening.

Everything is a happening for which neither you nor the other can be blamed. So even if a happening hurts, you cannot hate anyone, neither yourself nor the other. With the total acceptance of this concept, in an instant, your load of hatred for yourself (for your actions) and the load of hatred for the other disappears.

The absence of this load of hatred—both for yourself and for others—is the presence of peace of mind for yourself and a harmonious relationship with the other: the happiness you have been seeking all your life.

To Be Happy, Be Free From Any Image of Self

Satsang: Swami Sukhabodhananda

HESE days people are inclined towards glamour than goodness. Media highlights glamour. People are brainwashed to believe that glamour is equal to happiness. It is a wrong notion.

Why does glamour have more appeal than goodness?

There are three traits in human consciousness: looking good, feeling good and being good. The most important is being good. Many people value feeling good. However, if feeling good is not anchored on being good, then some people get into drugs. Drugs temporarily make you feel good, but are not good for your well-being. People also value looking good more because it helps to impress others. For them, looking good physically and psychologically is more important than feeling good and being good. There is nothing wrong in looking good provided it is based on being good. More often people want their image to be appreciated to feed their ego. Glamour is food for the ego; it decorates the looking good pattern. Hence, glamour is of greater appeal.

Is looking good wrong?

It is not a question of right or wrong. There exists a deeper meaning to it. A young girl, widowed at the age of 20, expressed that she was feeling lonely. I asked her why she could not remarry. She replied that she feared what people would say if she were to get married again. I asked her as to what people were talking about her right then. She replied that they felt that she was a good woman. However, I asked her if she was feeling good. In the eyes of the people she was looking good but she herself was not feeling good.

People sacrifice feeling good and being good for the sake of looking good. When looking good is not based on being good then life becomes a mess. The world runs on the illusion of looking good. If you do not look good, you will not survive this rat race, little realising that even if you win, you continue to be a rat. Are people happy in spite of being successful? Why is it that many successful people continue to be miserable? The reason being that they do not know the art of being happy. A study done on happy people showed that happy people were good finders. They always seek and find something good even in the bad.

Use the image of looking good but do not be used by the image of looking good. Just as you wear a dress, you are not the dress.

To be happy, be free from any image of yourself. Be empty of image, thoughts, and conclusions. This inner emptiness is joy. This is a new way of looking.

Why should I be a good individual if being good involves more problems?

People throughout the world want only good things to be spoken of them. Nobody wants others to talk ill of them. It is thus clear that we are all seeking goodness. Being a good individual requires facing problems. In fact, being a bad individual also involves facing problems. Problems are part of life, hence, train your mind to enjoy problems. Just as you go to a gym and enjoy the workout in spite of sweating, train your mind to enjoy problems. Problems often make you a powerful individual.

Guru Retails Bliss, Not Happiness

By Vithal C Nadkarni

 ARTIN Seligman had his Eureka moment when his five-year-old daughter accused him of being a grouch. He had just been elected president of the American Psychological Association and had criticised the child for being whiny, when she reminded the psychologist, renowned for his research on depression, not to forget how hard she had worked to stop whining. If she could stop whining, the child reasoned, why couldn't her father stop being grumpy? That's when Seligman realised that he, "a pessimist and a depressive of high critical intelligence", badly needed a 180-degree change of direction.

Positive psychology was born out of his new mission statement: to find out what makes life worth living as opposed to delving into what seemed to make it worthless. The difference was akin to that between a half-full and half-empty glass: one focuses on "plus" states with the same earnestness that the other brings to the study of "minus" states or negative emotions.

Traditional psychotherapy thus aims at converting acute human misery into bearable suffering while positive psychology promises to turn mild pleasure into a profound state of well-being, what the Czech writer Milan Kundera called "the unbearable lightness of being". Echoing an insight of eastern masters, positive psychologists warn, however, that you should not confuse this state with the garden variety of happiness that comes from, say, a sumptuous meal or climactic coitus. Instead, you need to separate "doing good" (sukarma) that leads to lasting happiness from "feeling good" which inevitably leads to a hunger or thirst (trishna) for more pleasure.

What positive psychology calls the "hedonic treadmill" could, therefore, be viewed as being equivalent to eastern tradition's endless rounds of Samsara. But there are radical differences too: unlike western purveyors of happiness with their pills and potions, eastern spiritual masters never try to make you "happy". For that would only condition you to a biological hit or "fix", with all its attendant downside dangers. Moreover, the aspects that positive psychology emphasises as worth cultivating—optimism, cheerfulness, gratitude, hope and spirituality—appear to be secondary add-ons of the existential bliss (ananda) flowing from liberation (moksha). Eastern tradition considers the latter to be life's ultimate goal. The realisation of your essential blissfulness (sat-chit-ananda) is, therefore, by definition a unitary state of incomparable fullness that lies beyond the dogmas and divides of opposites.

Critics of irrational exuberance also affirm that unlike happiness, bliss is not a station or a destination. They warn that we shouldn't make the mistake of thinking that we can "own" happiness just because it happens to be a noun. Happiness is a place to visit, not a place to live. Nor is equipoise (samatvam), eastern wisdom's prescription to attain bliss, the same as the euphoria obtained by the ebb and flow of the brain's feel-good chemicals. Potential disciples seeking spiritual wisdom of the East should heed a statutory health warning: the guru, who tends to speak in logic-defying koans, is a retailer of bliss, not happiness. Failure to make that distinction could lead the aspirant to crushing disappointment by missing out on happiness and bliss. Positive psychology would also do well to take on board the millennial insights of eastern wisdom and Oriental masters on their part need to share their techniques of attaining bliss and ecstasy for the benefit of humanity at large.

The Parable of the Blissful Madman

By Jahanavi Shandilya

HE Nobel Prize-winning mathematician, John Nash, who was in Delhi recently has a long history of schizophrenia, a mental condition in which the afflicted person creates a delusion of alternative reality. Schizophrenics do this to make so-called normal life bearable for themselves. Very often, those suffering from schizophrenia are creative geniuses. Apart from Nash, the long list includes musician Ludwig van Beethoven, painter Vincent Van Gogh, ballet dancer Vaclav Nijinsky and many others.

The life and works of gifted artists and creative geniuses show that their expanded consciousness is completely unconfined, giving rise to extraordinary potential beyond the reach of the average person. There is a tendency in the human psyche to reach for higher forms of consciousness. Access to this state is evident—though temporary—in both schizophrenics and individuals who get inspired by sudden insight.

Psychiatry has found no cure so far for schizophrenia and perhaps there is no cure. For, on a deeper level, it could be said of all of us that we are indeed schizophrenics in that the "normal" lives we lead and believe in, including getting a job, earning a livelihood, raising a family is, when seen from the plane of the spiritually enlightened, nothing but a carefully fabricated illusion very much like what schizophrenics construct for themselves.

So how do we break out of our delusions? Not necessarily by renouncing the world and all its illusory joys and sorrows, its fictive triumphs and tragedies, but by recognising the delusional nature of this world.

When we lose ourselves in meditation or in the exaltation that great music or art can create, the delusional world, with its myriad anxieties and griefs, seems to fall away from us and we feel a sense of untrammelled freedom. Nijinsky wrote in his diaries that he was God. This scandalised the pious Christian establishment of his time that considered such utterances as blasphemous. However, what Nijinsky had really done was to achieve, through the discipline of dance, spiritual liberation that revealed the transcendence within.

Nijinsky's story finds a parallel with that of the sage's response to a person who had come to see him for spiritual guidance, pleading that his everyday worries, cares, and daily search for meaning in life was driving him "mad". The sage heard him out and said: "I do not know if I can cure you of your madness, but right now you are an unhappy madman and I can transform you into a blissful madman."

It should be noted, however, that such spiritual prescriptions are not like over-the-counter drugs that can be bought and sold at will. True spiritual sages never offer a panacea for universal happiness, as distinct from individual bliss, because they know that such a thing is axiomatically impossible. It is only the individual seeker after enlightenment who can hope to ascend the spiritual escalator to an other-worldly joy.

"Unhappy madness"—of which schizophrenia is a severe form—is suffered by all of us who feel the constant pressures of the everyday material world. Blissful madness was what Nijinsky evinced or what the devotional Baul singers experience as do whirling dervishes who lose themselves in a frenzy of spiritual rapture.

Perhaps, that is why the form of madness we call schizophrenia or the more general form of madness called mortal existence cannot be "cured" but it can be transformed into the inspired, ecstatic madness of spiritual awakening. The other side of madness is not the so-called normalcy; it is the beatific insanity of bliss.

The Kindly Stranger To Your Rescue

By Jan Morris

I believe in kindness. Well, you may retort, who doesn't? But I believe in it rather as religious people believe in God. I think it is the answer to almost all our problems: from the miseries of divorce to nuclear proliferation. If humanity learnt to gauge its every action by the simple criterion of kindness—always to ask if it is, on balance, the kindest thing to do?—the world would be much happier... kindness offers us an uncomplicated morality, liberated from every species of mumbo-jumbo, the spells of witch doctors or the theology of professors.

The most striking manifestation of kindness is the kindness of strangers... The Kindly Stranger is related to the Righteous Gentile, the generic figure of Jewish tradition, who demonstrates that human understanding transcends even the grandest convictions of organised religion. The Righteous Gentile is, by definition, an outsider, or he would be just another Righteous Jew; and the Kindly Stranger is an outsider, too, or he would not be a stranger. The most celebrated was the original Good Samaritan, who came to the rescue of a mugged wayfarer on the road from Jerusalem to Jericho...Maybe, strangers feel compelled to help us just because they have nothing to do with us, and are reasonably sure they're never going to set eyes on us again. They are simply sorry for us, and pity can be the most easily satisfied of emotions—the more outlandish and lonely the sufferer is, the easier to satisfy it... It can be more difficult to be kind to friends than to strangers. Boredom, irritation, insight, disillusion, the broadening of experience, the sharpening of prejudices—all mean that sympathy can be hardest to cherish when you are dealing with the one you know the best, even the one you love the best. By definition, the Kindly Stranger must be alien to his beneficiary, but I have a disturbing feeling that the Kindly Friend, the Kindly Neighbour, the Kindly Relative or the Kindly Spouse might be a worthier subject of parable...

Kindness is really, so to speak, an absolute, which cannot be graded; but its most symbolical expression is the sudden, unpremeditated act of sympathy, offered without hope of reward to an unknown and perhaps unappealing soul in distress—to a foreigner, a truculent vagrant, an unwashed backpacker or a cat...

When, years ago, I was succoured in a bout of sickness by a Sherpa family in eastern Nepal, it was almost as though I was befriended by aliens. Few Europeans, if any, had ever been to their village in those days, and the smoky house in which I lay flickered mysteriously with butter candles around golden images, while women moved shadowily about, speaking in unknown tongues, and sometimes bringing me victuals from nowhere. The kindness of this family of strangers, though, was utter, and the fact that I didn't even know the local words for "thank you" made the experience all the more allegorical. It had a profound effect on me—I can still recapture the exact emotions I felt then, half a century later—and, fortunately, kindness is catching.

Nobody is kind all the time, but in the illimitable order of all things, in my view, every little bit helps. "Go, and do thou likewise", Jesus told his interlocutor at the end of the Good Samaritan parable, and perhaps if the charity of a stranger has saved us from ignominy far away, we are likely to be a little less testy ourselves when we emerge ill-tempered from a Himalayan fever.

(With permission from Lonely Planet: "The Kindness of Strangers: Travellers' Tales of Trouble & Salvation Around the Globe.")

Right Words Can Heal Your Heart

By Seema Burman

THREE words, "I love you," have changed lives miraculously while the three dreaded words "I hate you" have often triggered off violence. "Sorry", "please" and "thank you" have worked wonders. Some words can give you ulcers, heartburns or bruised egos.

Rahim, the poet, warned us against using rude words. He said, "Be cautious in speaking. When you injure another with your words the bond of friendship breaks forever. Even if the relationship is mended there will always remain a knot." So, beware of words. "Blind man's son is blind too," laughed Draupadi, when Duryodhana slipped and fell in the palace of the Pandavas, mistaking the glass floor for water. Draupadi's words of mockery set the stage for battle in the Mahabharata. However, harsh words cannot cause trouble if we refuse to react in a negative fashion. Says Sant Aasaram Bapu, "Do not let any one's harsh words govern your moods. Why should envy, fear, anger, lust, attachment and greed cause a storm in you? Be calm and you will always be happy. Only in a happy heart can spirituality unfold itself. To achieve self-realisation you must be happy and successful. To be happy is to be successful. Lust and anger destroy tranquillity and prompt us to run after illusory objects to gain a temporary feeling of satisfaction and a delusory feeling of fulfilment."

People are the same; they give back what they receive from you. Yet, day in and day out, people inflict poisonous darts on each other. Paramhansa Yogananda said, "When you feel tempted to speak harshly, control that impulse and talk calmly instead. Let no one hear harsh words from you. Be not afraid to speak the truth when you are asked to do so; but do not force your thoughts on others. You may be speaking the truth when you speak of a blind man as a blind man, or of a sick man as a sick man but be tactful so that sensibilities are not hurt. Some people turn sick with jealousy, others with anger, hatred and passion. They are victims of their emotions. You made your habits; you can change them."

In the Ramayana, Kaikeyi and Mantara were apprehensive of Sri Rama's return to Ayodhya after his 14-year-long exile. Realising their predicament, Sri Rama paid his respects first to Kaikeyi and only then went to meet his mother. He then spoke kind words and consoled Mantara and even asked her to continue living in the palace as before.

Kabir said, "Speak words that can make others forget their miseries. Utter words that can soothe others and which will also help you keep your cool." Chandogya Upanishad classifies four characters of the "mind-Brahmn" as nose, eyes, ears and speech. These are instrumental in taking the mind towards Brahmn. The organ of speech or Vag Indriya seriously distracts the mind. Observe mauna or a vow of silence at least once a week, said Swami Sivananda, as much energy is lost in talking. The energy thus saved becomes transmuted into spiritual energy. Will power becomes stronger, one becomes less restless, and a certain inner calm is achieved. This is the tapasya of speech. A disturbed mind can never be spiritually inclined. In the beginning, various thoughts force one to break the vow of silence. One has to be wary of such distractions.

The mind has to be occupied with positive thoughts. Restraining ourselves from speaking unnecessarily, requires considerable effort. Once inner tranquillity is achieved, mauna of the mind will come automatically. The mind becomes ready to meditate on Brahmn. Only he who can fix his mind on God, even if for two minutes, without distraction, can indulge in self-analysis. Books and gurus can only guide you on how to behave. Ultimately, it is you who has to gain control of your mind.

We have been gifted with the power of reasoning so that we can discriminate and exert self-control on our senses to evolve into better human beings. Lord Krishna, therefore, warns us, "Likes and dislikes of the senses for their sense-objects is natural. Let none allow himself to be swayed by them; they are his two enemies on his way to success." Krishna has said that these are the two foes, the gross expressions of the subtle vasanas or bondages in us, which can rob the seeker from perfection.

Metta Bhavna For Good Health

By S Krishna

 ETTA Bhavna is a Pali word meaning meditation of loving-kindness. The Buddha taught this meditation in Metta Sutta to 500 monks to cure them of their ailments and to protect them from evil spirits. Stanzas 4-8 of Metta Sutta say: "Whatsoever living beings there are; feeble or strong, may all beings, without exception, be happy minded. Let not one deceive another nor despise any person whatsoever in any place. In anger or ill-will, let him not wish any harm to another. Just as a mother would protect her child at the risk of her own life, even so let him cultivate a boundless heart towards all beings. Let thoughts of boundless love pervade the whole world; above, below and across without any obstruction, without any hatred, without any enmity."

Several accounts illustrate that by showing love and kindness, or simply by exuding thoughts of love and compassion, the violent natured can be made to become calm. The Buddha calmed the dreaded robber, Angulimal, and a mad elephant called Nalagiri by meditation of loving-kindness. A German baroness, Else Buchcholz, who became a Buddhist nun in 1919, tamed a leopard and a wild elephant in the jungles of Sri Lanka by radiating energy of loving-kindness towards them. Metta Bhavna is also practised to purify our mind of defilements like anger, jealousy, hatred and self-pity. We cannot stop the suffering of the world. We can only stop it in our mind, because we know our minds and we generate anger, hatred and jealousy in our mind.

The only way we can still our minds is by practising Metta Bhavna. Western scientists have found that 80 per cent of our illnesses such as rash, diabetes, backache and heart attacks are due largely to defilements caused in the mind. Psychiatrists have found that though there is temporary relief for these illnesses through medication, they recur because the cause remains within our minds. Whenever we feel negative emotions, they are first felt at the outer section of the brain, the cerebral cortex. About 13 billion nerve cells get activated on receiving these feelings and about 10 billion of these nerve cells are within the brain. Messages run across the nerves at a speed of 400 kmph. Immediately after receiving such a message, it gets transmitted to the hypothalamus, and to the nervous system, to the medulla of the adrenal in the kidneys. The secretion of four type of hormones start immediately, which make the body sick. These hormones are produced automatically, whenever we feel anger, hatred, jealousy, lust, greed and wrath. Thereafter, glucose is released from the liver to provide energy for activities such as fighting and running. Heartbeat rises to increase the flow of blood to provide strength in the body. Water from the skin and lips too is drawn into the blood. Many people experience dryness of mouth after anger and feel thirsty.

Frequent anger and hatred produce a chemical which reduces our immunity to illnesses. When we lose our kind thoughts and develop anger and hatred, immunity falls. Due to frequent negative thoughts, the mucus membrane in the stomach dries up, hormones are activated and excess pepsin enzyme is released into the stomach. The result? Ulcers. Our brain is hardly 2 per cent of our body size. But it uses 20 per cent of oxygen. Negative emotions have been found to use up more blood and frequent anger and hatred cause psychological ageing. Practice of meditation of loving-kindness can work wonders. British scientists have proved that meditation for loving-kindness restores chemical balance in the body and even cholesterol levels fall.

Look a Gift Horse in the Mouth

By Swati Chopra

WHEN the Christmas-New Year festive season is round the corner, we spin into a frenetic round of gift-giving. The act of exchanging gifts, however, has undergone a huge metamorphosis, from a personal, heartfelt offering to a commercial ritual, true to today's market mantra, which goads one to "shop till you drop".

"To give" may not always be the same as "to gift", although we often take one to be a synonym of the other. In giving is included the emotion of caring for and nurturing. Whether it is tending a love relationship like a garden or bringing up children, some of the most precious moments of our lives are ones in which we give of ourselves. When we share our deepest selves and take care of another, using our love and energy, this is the spirit that transforms objects into "gifts" and mithai into prasad. As the gold, frankincense and myrrh presented by the three wise men of the east to the newborn Jesus, that became sacred offerings when touched by the breath of devotion, and the fruit lovingly tasted for sourness by Shabri before she proffered them to her beloved Sri Ram. And, maybe, also the stick drawings we made as children and proudly gave our parents as cards. Unselfconsciously and simply, things become special when touched with love.

These days, most of us find it conveniently sufficient to give "of our possessions", on occasions deemed special by tradition and greeting card companies. While festivals like Diwali and Id-ul-Fitr have traditionally been occasions for exchanging gifts and sweets, this list has been added to in recent years with the inclusion of Father's Day, Mother's Day, Boss's Day and so on to our gifting calendar. These are times when we feel compelled to dip into our purses to show "how much we care".

Corporate gift-giving is one more phenomenon that this mindset has spawned. Gifts are given as extensions of business deals, often involving an unsaid quid pro quo arrangement. Both trends erode the natural giver who is hidden in the recesses of the human spirit. It is the part of us that rejoices in giving, that will enable us to give as freely as the flower that exhales its fragrance into the air for all to breathe. It is this natural giver that inspired us to concretise the urge to give into a religious duty: dana. If we paid any attention to it, we would find ourselves giving not because we have to or because we want something in return, but because it gladdens our hearts for we give in love. In this sense, giving need not only be something we do for others. It can be the way in which we reconnect with ourselves, too. Like the practice of meditation, that begins by acquainting us with the deep silence that lies at the core of our being, giving can become a journey into understanding the self and its deepest yearnings.

By becoming aware of why and how we would like to give, the act of giving may be transformed into a practice of mindful living. The warts need to be acknowledged as well in this process of becoming aware, including the recognition that at times, we gift as a form of material or psychological bribe, and even as an emotional one to gain the other's affection. We may begin this process at a very basic level, by contemplating gifts given to loved ones on birthdays and festivals. This can then be extended to other areas of one's life and integrated in acts of giving that form a part of all our lives—water to dry plants and thirsty animals, encouragement to young people trying to come into their own, care for the sick and the dying. Not only will giving in love then become the way in which we express ourselves in social relationships, it will also become the way we replenish and revere our spirit.

Altruism, Essence of All Knowledge

By Patwant Singh

I was asked to write a piece on spirituality, not religion—neither formal, scriptural, belief-based nor biographical. I have a problem with that. Which, quite simply, is: where do you draw the line between religion and spirituality? Doesn't one depend on the other for sense, sustenance and inspiration? Isn't spirituality largely refracted from religion? I believe it is another dimension, a condition, if you like, which owes its existence to the religious realm. Most of the world's major religions explain, in varying degrees of detail, the existence of things which are not susceptible to rigorous proof, like the occult, magical, astrological and supernatural phenomenon. But the enthusiasm and faith of adherents and their sense of spirituality makes them accept many things unquestioningly, without seeking further explication.

Sikhism does not believe in the magical, occult or supernatural. Based on rational thought, it does not require suspension of belief in the inquiring mind. In fact, enquiry and participation in the search for understanding the meaning of existence are encouraged. Because it is a republican and participatory faith, whose followers draw inspiration from the Guru Granth Sahib, the collected sacred writings of Sikhism's ten founding fathers, and other wise men of that period. The faith's religious beliefs and spiritual search are indistinguishable from each other, since both are firmly anchored in insights and logic provided by contents of the Granth Sahib, which opens with verses by Guru Nanak who founded Sikhism.

The tenth Guru Gobind Singh, before his death on October 17, 1708, ended the line of gurus by directing his followers to look upon the Granth Sahib—and not upon any individual—as their Guru thereafter. This, the Sikhs have done ever since. As a result, the collective wisdom of the gurus, saints and savants, and the philosophic vigour of their work, have guided successive Sikh generations for centuries, providing principled direction to sustain them through troubled times. By helping them renew their sense of determination, dedication and purpose. In turn, Sikhs have willingly sacrificed their lives to uphold the sanctity of their scriptures. In which realm would such a profound commitment to an idea fall? In the religious or the spiritual?

Nanak stated his belief unambiguously: "Religion lies not in empty words. He who regards all men as equal is religious." He insisted that Sikhs show a liberal and sensitive concern for the individual. To Nanak, God did not have a physical form, but was an ideal; an amalgam of truth, integrity and courage. So God was present in every person. Not the property of the priestly class, but of all humankind. And since God resides in each person, service of humanity was a form of worship. Voluntary sewa (or service), as a personal undertaking, is thus enjoined on every Sikh man, woman and child. It has become an ethical commitment for followers of this faith, without expectation of monetary rewards, or as a short cut to spiritual salvation.

Altruism is seen as the "essence of all knowledge". Sewa must be rendered in humility (nimarta), with purity of intention (hirda suddh), with sincerity (chitlae), in utter selflessness (vichon ap gavae), without desire (nishkam) and without guile (nishkapat). These attributes, sought to be instilled in Sikhs, were aimed at erasing distinctions between religion and spirituality, between the real and the abstract. Because there had to be an effortless relationship between the two, an inspired and acceptable co-mingling.

Guru Gobind Singh put the final seal of discipline and dedication on Sikhs by baptising them into the Khalsa. Although estimates vary, around 50,000 Sikhs were baptised during the first few days of April 1699 in a remote northern Indian town, Anandpur. In his message to the assembled Sikhs, Guru Gobind Singh told them: "You will love man as man, making no distinction of caste or creed... In each of you the whole brotherhood will be incarnated. You are my sons, both in flesh and spirit..." The emphasis on flesh and spirit was a reiteration of the idea of an inspired people knit together by their ideals and beliefs—by their sense of spirituality—in the fellowship of the Khalsa. Which is not a hierarchical order of the high above and the dispossessed below, but a humane, caring and courageous community.

Getting Connected With Compassion

By Anees Jung

THE 12/26 tsunami jolted one back to the mythical metaphor of the Old Testament when God unleashed 40 days of rain that flooded and washed away everything. In that apocalyptic moment came Noah's ark and the opportunity for creating a new beginning. A disaster like a tsunami probably signals the birth of a new understanding, believes Deepak Chopra who is baffled but happy to see the armies of the world diverting their activities from war to relief. "What may happen now will be true globalisation, not a globalisation of economic exploitation but one which has at its root the seed of compassion. Maybe nature is telling us 'I am giving you an opportunity to create a new humanity'," he says.

Once the disaster is relegated to history, will that understanding stay? "Then nature will react again till we get it. Or we destroy ourselves," says Deepak. "Turbulence in human consciousness at a collective level is somehow connected with the turbulence in nature. So nature's turbulence and our turbulence co-reflect and co-create each other. We contribute to the violence in nature and nature contributes to the violence in us. If we could heal the rift in our collective soul we may actually influence nature's activities." While thousands of humans perished in the raging tsunami, not many animals died, Deepak points out.

Two hours before the tide, elephants broke free of their chains and ran inland. So did wild bucks, buffaloes, and dogs. The birds started migrating two hours before the tide swept in. Why? Because they were connected. Deepak Chopra explains that the earth is a living organism. It has a collective consciousness and we are a part of it as is all life on the planet. Because animals don't have ego or a sense of a separate self, they feel the pain and anguish of mother earth. Humans have lost this connection.

Why don't we feel compassion when thousands die in conflict and war? "Because", says Deepak, "we demonise the other and see them as the enemy. Consciously or unconsciously or even through rigorous training, before people go to war, they mentally demonise the other. The tsunami is no demon and its victims are not our enemies. When you go beyond the demonised perception you discover a human being who is just like you. So compassion is possible when you put yourself in the position of the other. In the sharing of suffering, compassion is born; it is the flowering of understanding, love and healing. You cannot heal unless you heal the rift in our collective soul. At the deepest level of nature, compassion which is connectedness is a fact."

Deepak's son was travelling from New York to Los Angeles when 9/11 happened. "For eight hours I was in deep anguish... When I got a call from him I felt immediate relief. Five minutes later it occurred to me that people are feeling like this all the time—in Palestine, Israel, Northern Ireland, Bosnia, Sri Lanka, everywhere. Everyday parents, sisters, brothers, spouses and friends are feeling it. Why cannot I feel their pain? Because I haven't grounded myself in that field of consciousness. If I am not aware and I don't have creative solutions for problems then I have no right to call myself spiritual. Our measure of spirituality should be awareness and creativity, not puja-paath. To think of the tsunami as God's vengeance or wrath is a primitive notion. If there is a God we must attribute to him infinite awareness, infinite creativity. The abstract God is undefinable. It cannot be conceptualised. It is a luminous mystery."

Pass Around a Precious Gift This Season

By Janina Gomes

WO centuries ago when Jesus was born in a stable, innkeepers in Bethlehem had no room for Mary and Joseph. Pan to the year 2005. The situation hasn't changed much. Jesus is still being turned away by people who say they have neither space nor time. With contrived gaiety, artificial lights and noisy revelry, we tend to crowd him out. If only we look into the eyes of the neighbourhood orphan, reach into the heart of the destitute or sit in silent meditation, we can hear His voice.

Conrad Aiken said: "One cricket said to another: Come, let us be ridiculous, and say love." He was talking about the kind of love that is passed on in Christmas. Like diamonds sprinkled on a clear moonless sky or a rose petal that's tender to the touch. Like the tree outside our window that gives shade and sustenance to others or the breath of an infant child.

The ultimate gift that God gave us was to show us his face in Jesus. Yet, it is the true face of Jesus that people would rather flee from. That is because the gift comes wrapped in foils of hardship, pain, affliction, poverty and sometimes even disgrace. The wrappers so intimidate us that we hesitate to open the gift.

When the woman said: "I can't love anymore. With my love I have given away all that I am," the tree replied: "Look at me. There are robins in my branches, owls in my trunk, moss and ladybugs on my bark. They may take what I have, but not what I am." This is the unconditional love Jesus personified.

Human relationships have come to mean manipulation and control. Let's hark back to images of that first Christmas. They reflect love, awe, simplicity, humility and wonder.

Christmas Eve today will have images of plenty in some quarters, but unshared. There will be images of crowds and gaiety, but they will be exclusive, not inclusive. Churches might be packed for services, but the hearts of many would be still lonely.

Oscar Hammerstein asked: "Do I love you because you're beautiful or are you beautiful because I love you?" Once, a king tried to help a lost boy find his mother, who the boy said was the most beautiful woman in the world. So the king commanded all the beautiful women in the kingdom to come to his castle.

They came from far and wide: women with porcelain complexions, hair of spun gold, cheeks the colour of apricots and eyes as dark as the raven's. But none was the boy's mother.

When the last of the women had left, they heard a timid knock on the door. "Come in," the king said wearily. In shuffled an old washerwoman, her grey hair tied in a kerchief, her hands rough and red, her dress coarse and patched. "Mother!" the boy cried and leaping from his chair, raced into the woman's arms.

Christmas reminds us that to love is to create beauty. Love unconditionally and experience the love of Jesus. Pass it around.

Steer Your Mind To Selfless Service

Mata Amritanandamayi

BE always engaged in the service of people. The human body is anyway impermanent, so it is better it wears out in service. Constant effort and hard work are absolutely essential. If ten rupees is earned by hard work, we must return a thousand rupees to society through more hard work.

Prayer and worship are not enough. There is no difference between the Creator and His creation. Do you need to show a candle to the sun? Similarly, you do not need to worship God. He is within you and in everybody around you. In service to His creation, you establish contact with the Creator. Krishna, even though He was complete in Himself, still worked relentlessly. Arjuna, however, wanted to run away from the scene. You cannot run away. You have to do your bit. Not always will the situation be to your liking. You may not be able to change it. You can only change your mind, your attitude. If your neighbour makes too much noise, you can complain to the police. If your street is noisy, you can move elsewhere, but if your mind is creating all the chaos, what do you do? Recognise those circumstances we can change, and those we have to accept.

A king got pricked by a thorn when he was out hunting. He was furious and ordered that his entire kingdom be carpeted. His ministers were in a fix. Where from would they get so many rolls of carpet? A senior minister offered the suggestion that the king wear shoes and, thankfully, the king appreciated him. Similarly, we too should be able to change our attitude, we cannot expect the world to change.

How can we change our attitude? For that, mind control is important. Our mind is like an old car that stops only after colliding against some object, for its brakes don't work well. Modern cars come to a standstill the moment you apply the power brakes. The mind is like a supermarket with many thoughts. In a supermarket, we do not buy everything and anything. We take only that which we need. Similarly, we should let only some thoughts develop and let others disappear. The mind is like an elephant. An elephant, along its path, keeps plucking, tearing at any branch or leaves that come its way. But when the mahout keeps it on track, it is focused and walks a straight path. To still the mind and to have its remote control in our hands, we need meditation.

However, people meditate, do japa while their mind is travelling elsewhere. To steer the mind, you need to be aware, to be mindful. If someone were pointing a gun at you, how conscious you would be of yourself! It is that kind of alertness or awareness that we should have all the time. If we are close to fire, how careful would we be! That is how careful we should be with every moment of our life. The mind is like water, it is always turning downwards, weighed down by our many desires and worldly aspirations. Water always flows downwards. But look at fire, it always leaps upwards. If you put fire under water, it sends water also upwards in the form of steam. We should be like that. Our mind should be able to be light and alert.

As told to Sudhamahi Regunathan

The Act of Giving Spontaneously

By D M Sinha

HE disastrous tsunami has revealed different aspects of human nature—heroism and hope, compassion and charity—brought together actors, businessmen, spiritual leaders, NGOs, sportsmen, fishermen, politicians and other people from various backgrounds to reach out and help. What makes us respond thus to human tragedy, abandoning the safety and comfort we're used to, in order to lend a helping hand? And what is it that inhibits some of us from reaching out?

Seeing the enthusiasm of those who are performing seva would have gladdened Swami Vivekananda who had immense faith in people, especially the young. Tragedy gives rise to various opportunities as well; it creates the environment to make a fresh beginning.

What determines the way we react to disaster? Bhagavad Gita says that people act and behave in accordance with their innate nature. The difference in behaviour is due to the fact that actions done in pursuance of desires in the past propel us to do what we do in this life. This is what creates the innate nature of an individual and governs actions in this life. Knowledge acquired in this life helps purify the mind. The essence of karma yoga is that righteous actions done with dedication lead easily to self-realisation.

The basis of all righteous action is virtuous thought. Krishna has listed 26 divine qualities on which the edifice of righteous action is built. And among these qualities is daya or compassion and daana or charity. Compassion is empathy for those who are suffering and charity implies using one's material resources as well as the assistance rendered by imparting one's knowledge to others for love. Krishna says, "The divine properties lead to liberation and the demonic to bondage, O Pandava! Grieve not, for you are born with divine properties." The natural tendency of a being is to accept and foster the divine properties; this does not need any great input of effort. This is why Krishna asks Arjuna not to grieve, for the individualised self is by nature divine. Demonic properties like anger, harshness and arrogance are not the innate nature of any human being. Yet, one inculcates them due to wrong associations and beliefs, getting bound to endless births and deaths. Krishna explains that those having more sattvic qualities are attracted towards divine qualities while those under the influence of rajas and tamas are attracted to demonic qualities.

Dharma means a set of disciplines that enables us to hold on to sattvic qualities. Divine qualities fall in the category of dharma as righteous disciplines. Whenever a person performs his duty, his qualities are revealed in his actions. In this sense, duty is an important aspect of dharma and dharma indicates a particular path or philosophical dogma. It is a means of manifestation of one's potential divinity that may manifest itself in one as a mastery of scriptures, in another as expertise of military science, and in yet another as high business acumen. It is this manifestation of divinity that is known as God-realisation or Self-realisation. Whatever is spiritually ordained duty, born of righteous inclinations, must be done enthusiastically, even though its performance may mean facing formidable difficulties.

Krishna advises one to shed all conceit, of being a doer of actions through mind, speech and body. While performing duties, the sense of an action being superior or inferior has to be given up completely. The performer of seva must surrender himself unconditionally. Such action leads to godhead.

Significance of Giving Heartfelt Thanks

By Muhammad Ishaq Khan

HE act of expressing thanks to the Supreme Creator through prayers, charity and good acts is ordained for bringing an individual closer to an understanding of the purpose of Creation.

Thanksgiving has been highly valued in the Qur'an. "What concern hath Allah for your punishment if ye are thankful for his mercies and believe in Him? Allah is ever responsive, aware." The more a believer reflects on this Qur'anic verse, the more he is able to realise the depths of his growing spiritual consciousness that he is an inseparable part of universal consciousness. The primary objective behind the constant expression of thanks is in acknowledgement of gifts that Allah has bestowed on all human beings.

An expression of gratitude—also an act of thanksgiving—for small courtesies is part of our normal behaviour. Normally, most people thank each other in their daily conversation, correspondence and other forms of social behaviour. Life would be dull and dreary if we stop making friendly gestures in our human relationships. As a matter of fact, the development of both personalities and societies is in no small measure affected by our individual friendly actions and responses. It is not, therefore, difficult to understand why Allah wants our thoughts and actions to be in harmony with ethical principles of spiritual practice.

Any deviation from universal ethics recommended by scriptures and sages is bound to create disharmony in human relations; and this is why the Qur'an repeatedly brings home to us the significance of being conscious of our duty to Him and His creatures. "Seest thou one who denies the Judgment to come? Then such is the one who repulses the orphan, and encourages not the feeding of the indigent. So woe the worshippers who are neglectful of their prayers, those who want but to be seen, but refuse to supply even neighbourly needs."

Being poor or destitute is not a disqualification in spiritual terms. Likewise, any physical challenge does not disqualify an individual from remembering his Creator so long as he has consciousness. In modern times, the physically challenged have been able to overcome most of their limitations, thanks to individual efforts and technical aids. What is more, some of them have even won worldwide recognition for their individual achievements.

Hellen Keller distinguished herself as lecturer, author and educator despite being visually challenged and hearing impaired from infancy. About cosmologist Stephen Hawking, Time magazine writes: "Even as he sits helpless in his wheelchair, his mind seems to soar ever more brilliantly across the vastness of space and time to unlock the secrets of the universe".

Paradoxically, despite being of sound body and mind, many of those who are relatively less challenged in life tend to forget to express gratitude. Their inability or forgetfulness to express gratitude is a sign of weakness. Thankfulness indicates a disposition to express gratitude by giving thanks, as to the beneficent and merciful. There is often a sense of being delivered, liberated or salvaged as well as of thankfulness when a true seeker remembers bounties that the Creator has bestowed on him.

In fact, a thanksgiver's gratitude is the exemplification of his consciousness to realise that Allah is always ready to guide the one who submits to Him in all humility, earnestness and gratefulness in the hope of proving himself to be a true embodiment of spiritual and social stability and harmony.

Give Thanks: It's Part of Spiritual Evolvement

Discourse: Sant Rajinder Singh

OD once sent two angels to earth to gather the prayers of humanity. The first angel was asked to collect all those prayers that were essentially requests from people asking God for something. The second angel was asked to collect all the prayers of thanksgiving.

The two angels agreed to meet in a month with their collections. They began their task. The first angel, collecting prayers that appealed to God for something, became extremely busy. Several baskets were needed to hold those prayers—asking for more money, better health, bigger house, car, computer, jewellery and clothing. Some prayed for a spouse, for children, or for better relationships. There were so many such prayers that the angel had to obtain a van to cart them.

Meanwhile, the second angel travelled far and wide looking for prayers of thankfulness. Several days went by with hardly a prayer of gratitude heard. All that this angel heard were prayers asking for things.

A month later, the two angels returned to God. The angel collecting prayers for requests was laden with many baskets. The angel collecting prayers of thankfulness had only a few, a small amount compared to prayers requesting things.

The story illustrates the human condition. Many of us request others to do things for us, but how many of us thank them? Similarly, we pray to God for so many things that we want, but do we thank God? A similar situation is faced by parents and teachers. However, when there is feedback of appreciation, it is heartwarming for the parent or teacher to receive thanks from their children or students for what they do for them. It is not that they ever cease to sacrifice and serve selflessly, but it's nice to know that the gift of love they give is acknowledged and appreciated.

We are fortunate to be born as humans. Only as humans do we have the faculty to know ourselves and to realise God. For this, we should thank God every day of our lives. Once a man went to Heaven and God told him that he was lucky to have a human form. The man asked God, "Why are humans so special?" God first showed the man insects, birds, lizards and other creatures. "Notice that they all have their heads turned down towards earth." Humans can look up. They are the only ones that can lift their sights from the world to see God in the spiritual realms above. Human beings are blessed with a special faculty to gain spiritual knowledge. That opportunity is offered to every human being, but few make use of it. One needs to meditate to make full use of the gift.

By meditating daily, we can achieve union with God and realise that we are part of God. By meditation on the inner Light and Sound of God, we can slowly and steadily achieve true happiness and fulfilment.

Let us thank God for the many gifts we have received—for our birth, health, food, clothing, shelter and our families. Let us also thank God for our education and our jobs. However, let us not thank God merely with words but with deeds, by leading lives of non-violence, truthfulness, purity, humility and selfless service. Meditate daily so that we can connect with the inner Light and Sound which is the means by which we can turn to our true nature.

Day of Forgiveness and Thanksgiving

By Andalib Akhter

ESTIVALS have great value in human life. Occasional celebration of festivals breaks the monotony of our day-to-day life and brings cheer to all. For enjoyment and merrymaking, different religions have established specific time and dates. Islam, too, is not indifferent towards this joyful practice. Eid-ul-Fitr is one of the two annual festivals of Muslims, celebrated the world over.

Eid marks the end of Ramzan or fasting and is an act of collective thanksgiving to Allah for the reward of Ramzan and giving strength to the believers to keep fasts and worship for a whole month. It is a day of forgetting old grudges and ill-feeling towards fellow human beings. It is the occasion for showing joy for the health, strength and opportunities Allah has bestowed on us to fulfil his obligations of fasting and performing good deeds during the holy month of Ramzan.

Instead of commemorating an event from the past, Islam has prescribed Eid, the first day of Shawwal, the tenth month of the Islamic calendar, as an annual festival for Muslims when they undertake a great form of worship, the Roza. This is expected to remind a person that he should not rely on the accomplishments of one's ancestors but undertake virtuous acts to please the Almighty. Islam follows a unique approach in celebrating Eid. Islam has prescribed a simple yet graceful way to observe the festival. It is mandatory for all well-off Muslims to start their day by paying Sadaqat-ul-Fitr, an obligatory charity to the poor, so that they may enjoy the day along with others and may not be worried about earning their livelihood at least on the day of celebrations.

Sadaqat-ul-Fitr is an obligation for every Muslim, who owns 613.35 grams of silver or its equivalent, either in the form of money, ornaments, stock-in-trade, or goods beyond one's normal needs. Every person who owns such an amount has to pay Sadaqat-ul-Fitr, not only on his behalf but on behalf of his minor children as well. The prescribed amount of Sadaqat-ul-Fitr is 1.75 kg of wheat or money of the same value. This charity is given to the poor and needy. It cannot be adjusted in the wages of the servant, or be given for the construction of a mosque. It is advised that the Sadaqat-ul-Fitr is paid before performing the Eid prayer, but it can be paid before the Eid day. However, if a person has failed to pay on time, he should pay it as soon as possible.

After paying the obligatory charity, Muslims proceed to mosques or Eid Gaah to offer Eid prayers collectively. Here they present themselves before Allah, the Creator, and offer a special namaz or prayer to receive the blessings of the Almighty. During prayer, people from different strata of society stand shoulder-to-shoulder and bow and prostrate before Allah. All distinction of class and status disappear. After the prayer, they embrace one another and say "Eid Mubarak" to one another.

Since Eid-ul-Fitr is the day on which Muslims break their month-long fast, it is preferable to eat before going for prayer. Prophet Muhammad had the habit of eating an odd number of dates before going for Eid prayer. While going to the special namaz, Muslims generally do takbeer, or the glorification of Almighty as prescribed in the Qur'an, which says, "You should complete the prescribed period and then you should glorify Allah for having guided you so that you may be grateful to Him." The believer is expected to follow a particular guidance before performing the special prayers.

At the beginning of the day of Eid-ul-Fitr, one should wake up early in the morning and after a bath, he should put on new or best available clothes. After the namaz, Muslims are expected to celebrate the day in a responsible manner, greeting one another at home and in the neighbourhood. People visit each other's homes and partake of festive meals with special dishes, beverages and desserts. Children receive gifts and sweets on this special occasion. Islam advises not to violate the limits prescribed and never to indulge in acts that are prohibited, especially on this auspicious day.

Accept Good and Bad With Gratitude

From an e-mail forward

 Y family home was directly across the street from the clinic entrance of Johns Hopkins Hospital in Baltimore. We lived downstairs and rented the upstairs rooms to outpatients at the clinic.

One summer evening as I was fixing supper, there was a knock at the door. I opened it to see an awful-looking man. I stared at the stooped, shrivelled body. His face, lopsided from swelling, was red and raw.

Yet his voice was pleasant as he said, "Good evening. I've come to see if you've a room for just one night. I came for a treatment this morning from the eastern shore, and there's no bus till morning." He told me he'd been hunting for a room since noon but with no success. "I guess it's my face... I know it looks terrible, but my doctor says with a few more treatments..." For a moment I hesitated, but his next words convinced me: "I could sleep in this rocking chair on the porch. My bus leaves early in the morning."

When I had finished the dishes, I went out on the porch to talk with him a few minutes. It didn't take a long time to see that this old man had an oversized heart crowded into that tiny body. He told me he fished for a living to support his daughter, her five children, and her husband, who was hopelessly crippled from a back injury.

He wasn't complaining; in fact, every other sentence was prefaced with thanks to God for a blessing. He was grateful that no pain accompanied his disease which was, apparently, a form of skin cancer. He thanked God for giving him the strength to keep going.

At bedtime, we put a camp cot in the children's room for him. When I got up in the morning, the bed linen was neatly folded and the little man was out on the porch. He refused breakfast, but just before he left for his bus, haltingly, as if asking a great favour, he said, "Could I please come back and stay the next time I have a treatment? Your children made me feel at home. Grownups are bothered by my face, but children don't seem to mind."

I told him he was welcome to come again. And on his next trip he arrived a little after seven in the morning. As a gift, he brought a big fish and a quart of the largest oysters I had ever seen! He said he had shucked them that morning before he left so that they'd be nice and fresh. I knew his bus left at 4 a.m. and I wondered what time he had to get up in order to do this for us.

In the years he came to stay overnight with us, there was

never a time that he did not bring us fish or oysters or vegetables from his garden. From him, we learned what it was to accept the bad without complaint and the good with gratitude to God.

Recently, I was visiting a friend, who showed me her flowers. We came to the most beautiful one of all, a golden chrysanthemum, bursting with blooms. But it was growing in an old dented, rusty bucket. "I ran short of pots", she explained, "and knowing how beautiful this one would be, I thought it wouldn't mind starting out in this old pail."

"Here's an especially beautiful one", God might have said when he came to the soul of the sweet old fisherman. "He won't mind starting in this small body."

Shukriya, Dhanyavaad, Thank You Very Much

By Runjhun Noopur Dixit

AMONG the most oft-repeated words in our daily lives is "thank you". However, mechanical repetition of these words has robbed them of their essence: the heartfelt gratitude that the words seek to express. True thanksgiving goes deeper than mere words; it arises out of appreciation and gratitude—sometimes even for the gift of life—out of a sense of wonder and humility, acknowledgement and submission.

Most of us can narrate a number of incidents when these words are uttered distantly and impassively. But very few would be able to recount even a single incident in the recent past when a warm and heartfelt gratitude was either given or received. These golden words seem to have lost their true purpose and meaning in the hurly-burly of our busy schedules, leaving us with little time to think deeply or even from the heart.

Gratitude is more than just another emotion or expression of humility. It is an attitude, a way of life, even a gateway to a happy, positive and reassured life. Incredible as it might seem, this simple emotion has the potential to release positive forces like love, hope, compassion, humility, joy, reassurance and faith in an individual's life. In the material world, gratitude is like a smile. If sincere, it transmits immense joy to both the giver and receiver. A heartfelt "thank you" can introduce joy and happiness even in those domains where there is a very practical exchange of money and services.

An attitude of gratitude towards life helps us look beyond the material world and view life as the gift it truly is. It helps us focus on those little blessings of life which are otherwise either shrugged off or taken for granted. A loving spouse, affectionate children, supportive friends, fulfilling career—the blessings are different for different people. But most of the time, we fail to realise the importance of these simple blessings while we still have them, and end up valuing them only when we lose them or when it is too late. What we're left with is a lingering regret of never having cared enough.

Allowing ourselves to feel gratitude helps us experience the present and cherish the beauty of life. The impermanence of life and its gifts is a universal truth.

Gratitude is probably one of the most effective cures for that widespread affliction called negative attitude. No matter how bad a situation is, a person always has something or other to be thankful for. You have an unsupporting boss. Be grateful that you have an option to leave the job and start afresh. If leaving the job is no option, be grateful for having a support system of family and friends to see you through tough times. You lost a loved one. Be grateful for all the moments you could spend with him while he was around. The attitude to gratitude helps us keep faith and hope alive, even when we hit a real low. Most importantly, it dissipates those typical and unavoidable negative perspectives which often prove self-destructive in tough times.

The words "thank you" have the potential to change the course of your life. Listing out all the things you feel grateful for is a therapeutic exercise that is sure to chase away the most persistent blues. Say "thank you" for being alive and see the magical change these words bring in your perspective towards life.

Tribute to Parents Who Give Us Their All

By Saniyasnain Khan

HEN my beloved mother passed away, I went into a state of prayerfulness, deep thinking and contemplation. The experience was a reminder that there is very little time at our disposal and at any moment death can come calling.

Many years ago, my father said that only that person has truly taken part in a funeral who has actually felt as if it is he who is being buried. This means that he should feel that at any moment his turn can come, as if the counting has reached up to the last but one, and now it is his turn. Therefore, a visit to the graveyard becomes a source of awe and reflection and acts as a reminder of death.

However, we are so involved in worldly things that we never stop to think about the day which is fast approaching us. Prophet Muhammad said: "People are asleep, they will wake up only when they die." All of a sudden, death will bring you standing face to face with God, at which time you will be held accountable for all your deeds. That will be the moment you realise that what you were doing was one thing, and that what you should have been doing was something else. Prophet Muhammad once said that on the Day of Judgment, a man's foot will not move unless he has answered four questions: where he earned his money from, and where he spent it; how he spent his youth and how he used his knowledge.

The Creator has divided human life into two parts: the pre-death and post-death periods. The pre-death period is very short (like the tip of an iceberg) in comparison to the post-death period, which is eternal. The pre-death period is the preparatory phase in which you prepare yourself to become eligible to enter Paradise in the post-death period. This worldly life is a "test" for everyone, whether poor or rich, powerful or powerless, strong or weak. Man is required to pass in all these tests and trials by leading a need-based life rather than a desire and greed-based life, so that in the life hereafter, God allows him to enter Paradise, to live there forever in close proximity to his Creator.

On the death of a loved one, one should not go into a state of mourning. The Qur'an gives us great hope in moments of grief and loss. It says that God will reunite all righteous members of the family in Paradise. Moreover, if a member of the family has reached a higher level of Paradise, all righteous members of that family will be "upgraded", so that they may all enjoy eternal bliss and nearness to God. This idea gives great solace and acts as an incentive and encouragement to do good work and lead a pious and righteous life.

The Qur'an reminds us of our parents' painstaking care in our upbringing, especially that of our mother: "We enjoined man to show kindness to his parents, for with much pain his mother bears him, and he is not weaned before he is two years of age." Prophet Muhammad said that when a man dies, everything connected with him is cut off except three things: continuous charity, knowledge from which benefit is derived and virtuous children who pray for him.

So, what could be a more appropriate prayer for our parents than the following: "O Lord, bestow Your mercy on them, as they raised me up when I was little."

Belief In Brahmn Is No Longer Blind Faith

By Mani Bhaumik

RANSCENDING all theologies and denominations, humankind had a conviction in a creator-divinity, such as Brahmn. For aeons, we have deemed this divinity worthy of adoration and have directed our ardent prayers to it, making it the vessel of our hope. People accepted this with blind faith because it enriched their lives. Is the belief in One Source at the hub of all spiritual traditions a blind faith or is it grounded in scientific reality? There is remarkable support from quantum physics and modern cosmology that the oneness of all spiritual traditions seems to be the same oneness that science is now pointing to.

The idea that everything physical in this universe comes from one source is getting general acceptance among most physicists. In 2004, the Nobel Prize in physics was given, in the words of the Nobel Committee, for contributions towards the Theory of Everything. This rather audacious theory aims to show that considering all the fundamental particles and fields that make up—at least everything physical—this universe, you are nothing but different aspects of one single source. This year's prize is for discoveries in cosmology that allow us to glimpse the universe close to its very inception.

Have you ever tried to picture how vast the universe is? It's almost beyond our comprehension. Yet, the preponderance of evidences uncovered by cosmology point to a mind-boggling fact that this vast universe originated from a space much smaller than a speck of dust. In fact, from so small a space that we are as large compared to it as the universe is large compared to us. It now seems plausible that the oneness envisioned by the Theory of Everything existed at the inception of the universe in a tiny nugget of space. All these evidences give us reason to have confidence in the belief that at least everything physical in this universe comes from one source.

However, it still leaves a big hole in our scientific world view, since it fails to make room for our consciousness. Consciousness is the very window through which we perceive reality. So, we cannot push it aside as something unimportant. Eminent British physicist Roger Penrose forcefully argues that a scientific world view which does not profoundly come to terms with the problem of conscious minds cannot claim the pretension of completeness. Consciousness stares at us when we deal with the underpinning of our world that is the quantum world. Unfortunately, it is fashionable for most physicists to follow the cliche, "shut up and calculate", than to explore its implication more fully.

Nevertheless, if we look into it carefully, we find that quantum physics does pave the way for us to accept mind and matter as two irreducible but inseparable aspects of universal reality, just like the inseparable wave and particle aspects of a quantum particle. Even in classical physics, Einstein showed us that space, time and field are magnificently intertwined in their existence—they are inseparable. So, there are distinct examples of the co-existence of inseparable properties in the universe.

Pioneering physicist David Bohm went one step further. He envisioned the existence of a higher order of reality, which he called the implicate order. That is the universal source of inseparable aspects of consciousness and matter, where they cannot be distinguished. This cogent higher order makes it possible for us to comprehend the existence of true Oneness. Thus, belief in Brahmn is no longer a matter of blind faith; it is anchored in scientific reality.

Darwin As Avatar of Elective Consciousness

By Jug Suraiya

CHARLES Darwin's theory that humans have descended from the apes has long been assailed by Christian "creationists". Now, Darwin's theories are under attack by Islamic fundamentalists in Turkey as well.

In contrast, no one has made much of a fuss about Darwin in India. This is not surprising as most subscribers to the Indic tradition (which includes many who are not of the Hindu persuasion) believe in reincarnation. Never mind humankind, you as an individual may well have been an aardvark or a centipede in your last life, and could well be born again as a cockroach or a king in your next existential instalment.

Karmic reincarnation is a childlike parable. "If you eat while you're lying down, in your next life you'll be born a snake," a mother cautions a lazy son who has developed the messy habit of eating in bed.

But reincarnation is symbolic of far more than such mechanics of metamorphosis. (If I go on wilfully harming people in this life, my actions will cause me to be born again as a venomous creature, a scorpion, or a politician.) Such a literal version of reincarnation might work as a moral policeman to deter anti-social behaviour. The underlying subtext, however, contains an insight that goes far beyond the "self"-ish boundaries of individual crime and retribution. Reincarnation is an allegory for the inextricable interpenetrability of consciousness, all consciousness.

If you go about cheating and robbing, you will be reborn not in the next life, but in this very existence with the consciousness appropriate to a parasite, a bloodsucking bed bug. If you essay the higher levels of meditation, you will be reborn, here and now, with the consciousness of a Himalayan sage, or a soaring eagle whose eye reflects the blue arc of the all-encompassing sky. Reincarnation is really about elective consciousness. This is the metaphor underlying the 10 avatars of Vishnu: he is all of them, and none, at the same time.

In The World as Will and Idea, Schopenhauer reinterpreted the conventional theory of reincarnation by suggesting that the world as it exists is fashioned by the interplay of conflicting consciousnesses, with one prevailing and living on in the mode of the other.

In the German philosopher's view, one consciousness overcomes the other; in the larger Indic context each consciousness exists within the other. In a way, this is the aim of literature and other forms of art: not just the expansion of consciousness, but the realisation of the interdependence of all consciousness. For example, how could a septuagenarian Russian with a long beard reincarnate himself as a teenager going to her first ball? How did Tolstoy create Natasha in War and Peace and, in turn, was created by her? Who came first, whose being had priority? Who "descended" from whom?

Seen in the light of interdependent consciousness, the argument between Darwinism and creationism becomes a non sequitur. The question as to whether humankind descended from (was created by) monkeys or by God becomes irrelevant in the face of the counter suggestion of elective consciousness that God (and monkeys) could with equal validity be said to have descended from humankind. Evolution, seen as the reincarnation of elective consciousness, is a two-way street. If a King Kong forebear created Charles Darwin, the anthropologist equally created the ape. For both are manifestations of a common Creator, who is also their common descendant.

There's Order in Realms of Physics and Metaphysics

By G S Tripathi

 F all human values, truth and honesty contribute most in bringing about a certain order in life. These are also traits which make science—through experimentation and deductive logic. Scientists are as spiritual as other truth-seekers.

Science induces rational thinking and the spirit of inquiry. So, cultivation of science not only leads to material gain through resultant technology but also creates new knowledge beneficial for humankind. Progress of science takes place slowly, revealing the mysteries, beauty, symmetry and glamour of nature. A person of scientific temper experiences indirectly an internal strength which orders life.

Order results more from internal strength than from external induction. Spiritualists call it self-realisation. The degree of self-realisation determines the extent of order. In the following, I present few examples of order-disorder transformations in matter from a scientific angle and try to underscore the importance of internal mechanisms of order.

Consider the case of ice and water. The former has order in the arrangement of water molecules, while the latter lacks it. The difference lies in the concentration of molecules, which is higher in ice. Interaction among the molecules gives rise to order. Inter-molecular interactions are weak in water, where the molecules are less or more diffused. A person with a high degree of concentration has his senses controlled and focused to a great degree. An unorganised person lacks the necessary concentration for order.

A physically ordered state can be transformed to a disordered state if the cause for the order is weakened. Ice when heated loses order, because rise in temperature agitates the molecules, thus weakening the interactions among them. It is easy to convert an ordered state into a disordered one, however, the reverse is not always true. Similarly, an ordered person can be disordered once he loses internal strength. Of course, some degree of order or discipline can be induced in a person by external means. However, it lasts only until the external induction is effective.

A liquid, when cooled, may transform either to an ordered state or a disordered state of the solid, depending on the manner of cooling. If the cooling is slow, the resultant state would be likely to be an ordered state because the constituent atoms will find enough time to organise themselves. However, if the rate of cooling were fast, the resultant state would be again a disordered state. Similarly, an unorganised person can be organised depending on the manner and means of transformation. No wonder some people remain unorganised throughout.

Iron is magnetically ordered by an internal energy corresponding to a magnetic field strength of 1,000 Tesla below some characteristic temperature. Even one-tenth of this field has not yet been generated by external means.

Science has an important role to play with regard to bringing about order in life and to furnish scientific mechanisms of order-disorder transformation in both matter and life. While in the case of matter, the mechanisms are based on experimental confirmation, in the case of life, these are extrapolations to provide a scientific simile.

Two and Two Could Make More Than Four

By Rudrapatna Subramanyam

 A baby announces its arrival in the world with its shrill cries; a man announces his departure from the world by his unbroken stony silence. The book of life covering the period between birth and death contains pages of joy and sorrow, success and failure, triumph and tragedy, pleasure and pain, fulfilment and disappointment, health and sickness. Life is a mixed bag of pairs of opposites. Highs and lows are interwoven and form integral parts of the mosaic of Life.

It is our basic nature to seek happiness. Do we get it? When we look around, we find ourselves surrounded by suffering. We feel uneasy; that we are perched on an island of some happiness, surrounded on all sides by deep and dark waters of unhappiness. Is happiness just a mirage? The fact is that there is neither undiluted happiness, nor unabated unhappiness. Life is both. However, the nature of pain is such that it appears that the unhappy phase of life is interminably long.

When we are faced with unhappy situations, we may derive some comfort by observing and learning from Nature. A cold and dark night yields to a refreshing morning sun, with its soothing rays of warmth, radiating light dispelling darkness. After every chilly winter, there comes the spring, bringing warmth, hope and cheer. At the end of a dark, long tunnel, there is light.

Happiness is a state of mind, which keeps us in a state of well-being. Several important ingredients go to make the "commodity" known as happiness. But this precious commodity is simply not available in a departmental store. While money can buy pleasures, it cannot buy happiness. A rich man need not necessarily be happy. By the same token, a poor man need not necessarily be unhappy. Happiness has to be experienced from within. A fairly comfortable financial position, cordial and harmonious family relations and good health contribute to a happy life. But these alone would not ensure enduring happiness. Many a time we script unhappiness for ourselves and for others.

The mind reacts to external stimuli and this could sometimes bring us happiness or unhappiness. For enduring happiness, the internal war that rages within our minds should first cease. We should come to terms with external ground realities. As physical training keeps the body in good shape, similarly mental training helps in keeping the mind tranquil and balanced in the face of adversity.

Things happen not as we want them to, but according to a preordained scheme of things, over which we have little control. We were not consulted about the choice of our parents, place of birth, our sex. Neither will we be consulted about our time of death, its place and manner. The cards are dealt to us. We have to play them to the best of our ability. We do not gain anything by fretting or fuming over things over which we have no control whatsoever. We only become unhappy in the process. Accept gracefully the things given to us, the good or bad, and abjectly surrender to the dictates of destiny.

Life does not lend itself to strictly scientific analysis. In the rough and tumble of life, two plus two may not necessarily equal four. There are many questions for which we have no answers.

Human Behaviour Through the Prism of Science

By G S Tripathi

SCIENCE is beyond the grasp of many, mainly because it is perceived to be complicated. However, a closer inspection of some of the laws and phenomena in science would reveal how certain types of human behaviour can be interpreted through them.

Consider first the impact of education on students. We observe that education has an immediate impact on some, but for others, its impact appears much later. There is an analogy of this difference in behaviour in the phenomenon of luminescence. It is essentially emission of light by a body after it absorbs light from an external source. Absorption of light is a quantum phenomenon. There are two types of luminescence: fluorescence and phosphorescence. Fluorescence is emission of light by a body as soon as it absorbs light. However, in the case of phosphorescence, there is a time lag—from a few seconds to a few hours—between absorption and emission. There are bodies that absorb light but never emit it. For example, a piece of rubber absorbs light but never emits it. Some despite education never shine.

All virtues can be said to hinge on perseverance. Many things can be obtained by persistent effort. Progress is directly proportional to effort. However, the cause and effect are linked by a parameter, "obstacles". There would be progress if either the efforts are more or obstacles are less. We can understand this with Ohm's law, which states that in an electrical circuit, current is directly proportional to the applied voltage. Here, the connection involves a parameter known as resistance. Current would be more if either the voltage is high or resistance is less. This phenomenon is called normal conductivity. There is an extraordinary situation in this phenomenon, superconductivity, which is characterised by, among other things, a resistance-less state. This phenomenon occurs under specialised conditions and it has been observed that these conductors show persistent current even after the applied voltage is switched off. The impact of ordinary life is felt as long as it is related to an issue which has current relevance. However, the impact of an extraordinary life continues forever. In other words, lives of great men inspire us, for all times.

We experience strain if an external stress is very high, or if we are exposed to a small stress repeatedly. This is known as fatigue and it results sometimes in catastrophic conditions without prior warning. Similar phenomenon occurs in material objects and these show sudden breakdown. However, with care and regular inspection, these catastrophic conditions can be avoided.

The stability of material bodies depends on both attraction and repulsion. Consider common salt or sodium chloride. The electrical charges residing in the sodium and chlorine ions are opposite in nature. Hence, they should always attract each other. However, when these come closer because of attraction, collision and instability are prevented due to repulsion, which sets in at close distance. The stability of a relationship, likewise, depends on a judicious balance between attraction and repulsion.

Through these examples we could explore the unity between life and matter. The quest of science, so far, is to unite the smallest, starting from an atom downwards, to the largest, the universe. However, it has begun to extend to such diverse topics as the mystery of life, complexity of social behaviour and financial complexities. These evolve commensurate with the challenges of time.

There's More to Gut Feeling Than We Thought

By Narayani Ganesh

E may not be entirely human, say gene experts studying the DNA of hundreds of different bacteria in the human gut. They estimate that 90 per cent of cells in our body are bacteria.

Give or take a few hundred micro-organisms and you'll find that we're a mobile ecosystem, teeming with life. Bacteriological studies only confirm what mythologies from round the world have been trying to tell us: microcosm and macrocosm are inseparable, the one cannot do without the other. Together, they complement the evolutionary process of the entire universe.

We couldn't live without good bacteria that keep out the bad ones, as they contribute to essential body functions like digestion and immunity. "We are symbiotic organisms, relying on one another for life itself." This yin-yang, positive-negative flux is what nurtures life, as is evident from a study of any ecosystem—wetlands, coral reefs, deserts, fresh water or even ponds. The gut is a small example of the interplay of the many to sustain the one. This could be why indigenous philosophies respect all life, without exception. Those who live close to nature know instinctively—through gut feeling—that disturbing or removing even one constituent of an ecosystem would throw the entire system asunder.

In Nepal, the snake is associated with the sacred tree that is believed to hold the universe together. Killing or injuring a serpent, therefore, will not be viewed kindly. The stories and idioms might be different, but similar perspectives are found in most cultures. In India, the Bishnoi community continues its tradition of protecting wildlife. In Bastar, Chhattisgarh, it is a piece of (sacred) wood that is taken out on procession during Dussehra, the forest being integral to the lives of people. Snakes, animals, trees and the elements as objects of veneration/worship are symbolic of the intricate and interconnected web of life.

Myths interpreted from an ecological perspective can help create awareness of the symbiotic nature of all relationships and the importance of practising moderation in all we do to avoid upsetting the delicate, survival-friendly natural balance. Buddhism, Jainism and other pacifist philosophies promote compassion and non-violence as these help in achieving internal and external harmony.

James Lovelock's Gaia hypothesis looks at the Earth as a

super organism. The human body too, like other forms of biological life, is a kind of "mini" super organism made up of myriad living cells. In Tanzania's Serengeti National Park—and in many other such parks in Africa—the remains of dead trees are left undisturbed. For the dead tree becomes the habitat for an entire new ecosystem. Once dead, the human body begins to decompose soon—dust unto dust—whereas the dead tree continues to give life.

One of the findings of the Human Genome Project was that a lot of human genes—almost 90 per cent of the total—had no apparent purpose. They were dubbed "junk" genes. Later studies, however, revealed that junk genes were not junk; they were an integral and influential part of the genome. Piecing together the microcosm might never really get complete since to make sense of the parts is a very complicated process. We might never know how the parts make the whole. Yet, we do know that they're interconnected and that's what matters.

Faith Stranger Than Dan Brown Fiction

By Jug Suraiya

N the storm of controversy surrounding the film version of Dan Brown's bestseller, The Da Vinci Code, the one remark that struck me as being most appropriate was made—appositely enough—by a spokesman for Opus Dei, the supposedly "hushhush" Catholic order which features in the thriller. The Opus Dei representative has been quoted as saying: "The truth of the Christian faith is more interesting, more mysterious and beautiful than this fiction." I consider myself to be an atheist, but I couldn't agree more. Except that I would have enlarged the remark to include not just the Christian but all faith, and not just Brown's fiction but all fiction. But first let's look at The Da Vinci Code vis-à-vis Christian belief. Brown, who "borrowed" his central thesis from an earlier book called Holy Blood, Holy Grail by Michael Baigent, Richard Leigh and Henry Lincoln, claims that Jesus married Mary Magdalene, and that their progeny went on to found a royal line that survives till today.

Sensational stuff. Many would say—and are saying—it's more than just sensational, that it is slanderous of Christian faith. But compared to the central tenet of Christianity, Brown's potboiler is a damp squib. A nine-day wonder that doesn't stand a chance against the awesome might and mystery of a faith system whose reverberations resound 2,000 years after it was formulated. What is that tenet? That the Son of God could be born in the guise of a flesh-and-blood mortal, suffer crucifixion and undergo the miracle of resurrection to redeem humankind. It's not a bombshell of a plot; it's a thermonuclear explosion. No sensation-seeking thriller writer could have had the imagination or the nerve to dream it up. And even more profoundly mysterious and baffling than the Christian credo is the phenomenon of faith itself.

Asked what was the greatest mystery in the world, Yudhishthir replied: "That, when he sees death all around, man can still live each day as though he were immortal." Yudhishthir's point is that this is a faux faith, a specious immortality born of ignorance. But true faith—the faith of millions of Christians or Hindus or Buddhists or Muslims the world over—is the path to true immortality in a cosmic order beyond the mortal shackles of the illusion of an individual self, or ego.

But where does this eternally indestructible faith come from, and why does it choose as its repository the soap bubble ephemerality of the ego? Is faith—in a Creator, in moksha, in nirvana, in the transcendence of illusion—itself an illusion, a psychological contrivance we have devised to escape the despair of inevitable extinction?

Faith—in order to be faith, as opposed to proven knowledge—cannot be validated except in and through itself. It cannot rationally or logically be apprehended. That is the unplumbable majesty and mystery of faith. Shipwreck all you know on the reef of rationality, then take a leap in the dark to faith, said Kierkegaard. Faith is the leap in the dark, the ultimate cliffhanger to end all cliffhangers. Voltaire said if God did not exist we would have had to invent him. But if we did not exist, faith would have had to invent us. For who else but we, with "the scandalous audacity of nothingness", could believe in the unbelievable, could have faith in faith?

The Source Is Still With Us, Say Science and Religion

By Mani Bhaumik

CIENCE and technology have improved our lives by giving us material abundance. But science has also provided us with weapons of mass destruction. We need spirituality, more than ever, to generate a feeling of cosmic kinship for the survival of our species, as much as it has always been essential for an abiding personal happiness.

Spiritual traditions have been based on the oneness of creation. Can science today, in some manner, attest to our belief in the One Source at the hub of all spiritual heritage? Amazingly, the same scientific method that once compelled us to question the existence of God is now, by way of new physics and cosmology, developing evidence that tend to support our age-old belief in the One Source, a higher power behind all creation. We find remarkable support that the oneness of all spiritual traditions is the same oneness that science is now pointing to.

If the knowledge that everything in this universe comes from one single source takes root in our consciousness, can you see the profound impact it would have? Doesn't this mean that humanity is of each other? It really shouldn't make any difference whether you are black, white, brown or yellow, whether you are a Christian, Jew, Muslim or a Hindu. Yet, we see these differences are causing gruesome conflict in the world today. We desperately need the feeling of cosmic kinship that results from the realisation that everything comes from one single source.

Just like the God of religion did not leave the universe after creating it, science shows us that the source is still with us. The Star War movies made the phrase popular: "May the force be with you." In light of the discoveries of modern science, we can say that the source is always with us. It is up to us to get in touch with the source and give our mind a laser-like focus to realise our full potential.

Fortunately, the human brain has evolved to a point where our consciousness facilitates experiencing our oneness with the source, a higher power behind everything that people call God. This experience of oneness appears to have inspired the founders who started the great spiritual orders or religions of the world. Now, we can observe the brain scans of people who are in the state of consciousness when they experience the oneness and find that there is a distinct, repeatable brain pattern involved with the experience.

To those who experience the oneness, it is as real as any other experience when they are in their most alert state. When we take into account the fact that the same consciousness also enables us to infer empirically that everything comes from one source then it stands to reason that there exists the one source in reality that the brain is allowing us to experience.

Wonderful things can happen when we are in tune with the source within us. There is plenty of scientific evidence to prove that our consciousness can heal our body. Stress is the biggest killer in our society today. It causes disease and leads to disease. But if we are in tune with ourselves, we are in tune with nature and in tune with the one source of everything. Then our stress dissolves and we instinctively know the right thing to do. We feel blissfully happy and see ourselves as whole and one with the universe.

Really Speaking, There Are No Scientists Or Seers

By Jug Suraiya

S the paper that you are reading really a paper—or any "thing" at all—or is it merely the "appearance" of a paper? Further, are "you" really you, or just another "appearance"? Such questions could be put to you not by another-worldly spiritual seer, but by a very matter-of-fact scientist. Indeed, scientists are increasingly asking whether "matter" or "facts" actually exist in and of themselves.

Investigations of the subatomic world have shown that what we in the everyday world take to be tangible matter—this newspaper, your hand holding it—is largely composed of emptiness. All material things—a flea, an elephant, an ice-cream cone, Mt Everest—are made not of discrete particles—like tiny bricks—but of "events" which slip in and out of existence and are inseparable from our consciousness of them. One way of looking at it is that they "exist" because we perceive them to exist. Contrariwise, do "we" really exist other than by and through our act of perception?

So, if all matter is illusion, or at heart insubstantial, why is it that your hand does not go straight through the appearance of the paper you're reading? Or, conversely, why doesn't the paper go through the appearance of your hand? The scientist would say that is because though matter is insubstantial (not made up of any finally irreducible substance), it is held together by interwoven force fields, or "relationships" between the "events", that make up the unfolding narrative of the universe. This is beginning to sound not like physics but metaphysics, specifically Buddhist metaphysics that talks about samskara, the world of appearance or phenomena, of which we are an inextricable part, and which is based on the principle of total interdependence. (This paper is a paper because you are a reader, and you are a reader because it is a paper.)

The interdependence of all phenomena is the underpinning of the Buddhist concept of universal compassion. If all phenomena—a grain of sand, a galaxy, Salman Khan, a blackbuck—are part and parcel of the same shimmering interplay of appearance, it is not so much "morally" wrong to seek to harm another entity as just plain illogical because what you are trying to harm is only a reflection of you and vice versa.

A seer might call it the interdependence of all phenomena. A scientist might term it as Heisenberg's principle of uncertainty, by which through seeking to discover, we change what is sought to be discovered. A poet, who deals in metaphors, might describe it as interpenetrative consciousness. A metaphor is a way of interrelating two apparently dissimilar phenomena. "Shall I compare thee to a summer's day?" A metaphor is a bridge, a force field, which links together two or more seemingly disparate phenomena: one's beloved and the warmth and splendour of sunlight. The poet's job is to reveal such linkages, which is why Octavio Paz described a poem as a cosmos complete in itself, as "real" as the universe "out there".

So, is this paper that you are reading, really "real" or "really" just an appearance? A scientist, a seer and a poet might give three separate answers, which are but one. Just as are the poet, the seer and the scientist. And this paper, and you.

A Physicist's Faith In Science & God

By Charles H Townes

NO one can deny that the universe is the outcome of intelligent placing. It is unusual. We, too, are unusual. To make it possible for life to exist, special physical laws are required. So I would say that this is a very special universe. It has been intelligently planned. How can anyone confute that?

So, there is indeed a spiritual world; a Creator. Most people do not realise that science, like religion, requires faith. We make so many assumptions. We believe that the laws of physics are reliable—that's a kind of faith. We create experiments that can test and verify these laws. God initiated the universe, He created it. But we change the world too. Therefore, we have a responsibility; we have to ensure that we change it for the better. Take cloning, for instance. We humans are co-creators. How we go about cloning depends on whether we're doing it for the common good. It raises many complex and difficult questions. We are changing all the time. So instead of imposing a total ban on creative research, it is better to regulate it carefully.

What does technology do? It enhances our ability to do newer and bigger things—for good or bad. Then again, we can harm one another even without the help of technology. So the potential to hurt each other predates any technology. Science and technology merely enlarge the scope, the possibilities. The choice remains with us as it did even before we invented technology.

Science attempts to understand how the universe works. Religion attempts to understand the purpose and meaning of the universe. If there is purpose and meaning, it will affect the nature of the universe. Once we understand the meaning, we can get to know the purpose. Science is said to be objective while religion is subjective.

Science has its inconsistencies. Religion has its puzzles, too. Science doesn't allow free will; yet, we think we have free will. We have to learn to accept inconsistencies in both science and religion. The more we understand about the two, the greater the possibility of bringing the two streams of thought closer together. To make this possible, science and religion will have to change in many ways. True, science has many inconsistencies. Even general relativity and quantum mechanics are not consistent with each other. Yet, we think each one of them is correct. So too in religion. Now take the subject of revelations.

It is part of the history of religion. But revelations happen in science, too, except that a revelation is not called a revelation—it's an idea, a flash of genius, a new creation.

When the idea for the laser came to me, I was sitting on a park bench, thinking... why haven't I been able to do this? Suddenly, I got this new idea. Who gave me this idea? God? Who knows? In science, we don't usually talk about it. You could say I had an idea. I do believe there is a spiritual presence in the universe. It is difficult to define God, but I can feel an omnipresence everywhere. People ask, if God created the universe, who created God? So there's always a problem with a beginning. Many of us create a spiritual universe that is not visible.

This will evidently not be included in the domain of science. So too, free will. It is said that because we don't know, it can't be. I would say that because we don't know, we don't know.

(The author, a Nobel laureate, invented the maser and co-invented the laser. He spoke to Naryani Ganesh.)

Mapping the Physical and Mental Universes

By Narayani Ganesh

F the manual of life is encoded in our DNA, where do we look to find the blueprint of consciousness? This was a subject that fascinated Francis Crick, who, along with James Watson, discovered the double-helix structure of DNA 50 years ago. Engrossed in the mysterious relationship between mind and body, Crick later felt impelled to turn his attention from matter to mind and from biology to philosophy, but he persisted in believing that one day, consciousness could be explained in biological terms, using the tools of neuroscience.

The human genome map reveals to us that we're made up of some 40,000-odd genes, each of which carries inherited information. So, say some, we're the sum of our genes. It seems, however, that we could well be that and more—a combination of nature and nurture, matter and mind. But what is mind, besides the countless neuron cells that transmit nerve impulses through the complicated nervous system? And neurons are not confined to the brain—their reach extends to even the stomach and intestines. So Crick would often pose an intriguing question: "When you digest your lunch, is that you?" Crick questioned the hypothesis that there was a line dividing the functioning of the body and mind—he preferred to approach the question of consciousness through neurobiology.

Consciousness and awareness are essentially local phenomenon, generated by activated neurons, said Crick. He did concede, however, that with our present (limited) understanding of neural correlates, it would be impossible to prove it scientifically. Crick also admitted that it would be difficult to explain to others the nature of any conscious experience, without talking about it in relation to other such experiences. But since consciousness is subjective, science alone—which is objective—cannot fully explain the inner life of the mind.

This is the information age, thanks to the giant leaps we've made in computer chip technology. David Chalmers, of the department of philosophy, University of Arizona, raises a complex futuristic question: if the precise interactions between our neurons could be duplicated with silicon chips, would it give rise to the same conscious experience? Can consciousness arise in a complex, synthetic system? In other words, can consciousness some day be achieved in machines?

"Consider a silicon-based system in which the chips are

organised and function in the same way as the neurons in your brain. That is, each chip in the silicon system does exactly what its natural analogue does and is interconnected to surrounding elements in precisely the same way. Thus, the behaviour exhibited by the artificial system will be exactly the same as yours. The crucial question is: will it be conscious in the same way that yours are?" asks Prof Chalmers.

The synapse does not explain everything. Whether artificial intelligence can evolve to the extent of human consciousness or not, the fact remains that the many conflicting theories of the universe are not confined to the physical: we live in individual universes of the mind, too. If retraction or reversal of cosmological principles—Stephen Hawking recently revised his theory of black holes—are acceptable in the objective realm of science, so too should it be in the subjective mental universe.

If our perceptions of the subjective and objective universes are in a state of constant flux, it follows that theories of everything that seek to explain the A to Z in either domain will necessarily be in a state of constant evolution. And so we, too, will constantly be in search of an elusive truth...

Prevent the Influx of Karma Particles

By Kailash Vajpeyi

HE word Jain has been derived from Jina, which means conqueror, implying one who has overcome all human passions. The Tattvarth Sutra, a book of supreme wisdom, was written by Umaswati, Kundkundacharya's disciple. The opening aphorism of Tattvarth Sutra talks about enlightened faith, knowledge and conduct leading to final emancipation. The enlightened faith comprises jiva or life, ajiva or non-life, asharva or flow of karma, bandha or bondage of karma, samvar or shedding of karma particles and moksha. The enlightened faith is an awareness of reality or truth. It also means having unwavering faith in the words of Jainas. In certain cases, enlightened faith is also obtained by intuition. So is the case with knowledge which includes scriptural knowledge as well as knowledge obtained by intuition. Enlightened conduct means a determined effort towards spiritual life-journey.

Jainism has its unique theory of conduct and karma. Our good or bad deeds generate minute particles or atoms which bind themselves to and pollute the soul. The influx of these karmas can be stopped only when we prevent the influx of temptation. This is enlightened conduct. The shedding of karma is wiping clean old accumulated particles of previous deeds. Bondage explains the mechanism and arithmetic of karma particles. Moksha requires not only the complete wiping out of one's karmas, but also the acceptance of suffering to attain kaivalya.

Knowledge is divided into five categories—sensory or empirical, verbal or articulate, clairvoyance, telepathy and omniscience. The second aphorism is explained by Umaswati— consciousness distinguishes between living and non-living, emancipated and "bound" souls. Plants, animals, humans and other life forms fall in the category of bound souls.

The third and fourth chapters describe Jain cosmology: the shape of the universe resembles the three-dimensional figure of a man standing with his feet apart. The central cylindrical part is the dwelling place of all "mobile life". The peak of the universe is the abode of liberated souls or Siddhashila, below which lie abodes of celestial beings. The central hemisphere is the living place of all living beings. The Meru mountain lies at the centre; the lower part is inhabited by hellish beings. The fifth aphorism says that within the universe, both space and matter are non-sentient entities. Matter is governed by the law of motion and the law of rest. The universe itself has no motion and neither medium has any knowledge or consciousness.

The sixth aphorism says the activity of body, speech and mind is yoga which includes the joining of karma with the soul. All deeds and thoughts, negative and positive, result in the influx of karmic particles. So, Jain yoga is more difficult to observe and maintain. The influx is of eight types: jealousy, withholding knowledge, obscuring influx with vision or view (asrava), state of happiness induced by material circumstances, craving for beauty or fame, prestige, imbalance in daily conduct.

Chapter seven deals with five vows: shunning violence, lying, stealing, incontinence and possessiveness. A strict observer of these five vows often wishes for death during meditation or sanlekhana. The eighth aphorism enumerates the causes of bondage: wrong faith, non-abstinence, carelessness, passion and activities of body, speech and mind.

Once all obstructive karmas are destroyed, liberation can be attained. Then, the soul goes straight to the top of the loka (space occupied by the cosmos) and rests in eternal bliss.

Karma and Predestination Are Not Contradictory

By Ravi Panwar

HE law of Karma is postulated as follows: "As you sow, so shall you reap." The "reaping" is implied across several lifespans and not necessarily during the one in which "sowing" is done. You are the architect of your future. Clearly, this law is a call for right action in order to ensure a bright future. The theory of predestination, on the other hand, states that the future is predetermined. The question arises: why then should we struggle to carry out right action? We might as well relax and enjoy life.

On the face of it, it seems the two notions of karma and predestination are contradictory, insofar as their implication towards calling for right action is concerned. But is this really so? Person A is told that if he takes Action 1, he shall be rewarded; but if he takes the comparatively easy alternative, Action 2, then punishment awaits him. Clearly, these conditions should motivate Person A to take Action 1. Now, we introduce Person B, a close acquaintance of Person A. In fact, he knows the psyche of Person A so well that he can precisely predict his choice in the given scenario. Person B writes down on a piece of paper what action Person A is expected to take and folds it up. Sure enough, Person A takes just that action and is rewarded/punished accordingly. At this juncture, Person A opens the paper and lo and behold! He finds his pre-ordained future action revealed to him.

In the above example, can we say that the motivation associated with the reward for right action (Action 1) for Person A was in any way reduced just because Person B could predict his action in advance? There appears to be no rational basis for coming to such a conclusion. Extrapolate the example to theories of karma and predestination. Person A represents human beings while Person B, God, credited with being omnipotent, omnipresent and omniscient. Omniscience should logically imply knowledge of the future, since God is believed to transcend time. But proponents of "free will" would object to this interpretation. Let us then grant to God full knowledge of at least the present. Specifically, that He knows completely the psyche of each human being as also every set of circumstance that exists in the present moment. And, therefore, he can predict with absolute certainty what action each individual will take at any point in time.

Now, assume the law of karma to be in operation. Since God,

being omniscient, knows what man will sow at any instant and the law of karma rigidly ties what is sowed to what is reaped, it follows that God knows what will be reaped by man in the future, even before the sowing is done. God, then, is in a position to record the future with absolute certainty. Man's future is, thus, predetermined.

So, there is no inherent contradiction between theories of karma and predestination. Predestination appears to so strongly support the cause of easy-going people because it is often overlooked that, while the future may be predetermined, it is known only to God, since God alone knows the psyche of man fully, better than man himself, which, in fact, gives rise to the notion of "free will", seen from the point of view of man. The only thing man knows is that the law of karma is in operation. Against this backdrop, every rational individual would be motivated to carry out right action, notwithstanding an assumption of predestination.

Remove Blockages and Transform Your Life

By Zhi Gang Sha

PIRITUAL blockages are the result of mistakes of previous lives and also current life. These are "te" or bad karma; harmful acts and even thoughts that you create will add to your bad karma. All aspects of one's life are recorded in the Akashic records, or the Book of Life, which contains the history of every soul in the universe since Creation.

Service that benefits humanity and the universe is categorised as good karma and those that harm, as bad karma. A person with good karma will receive divine blessings. Bad karma, however, is the root of blockages and disasters.

You may or may not believe in karma. I am merely sharing my knowledge and views on the subject. As human beings in the physical world, we are subject to laws of our country, state and city. When we break these laws, we may become involved with lawyers and judges. You may not realise that every soul is subject to the spiritual laws of the universe. And, just as there are lawyers and judges in the physical world, there are lawyers and judges (so to speak) in the spiritual world too. The effects of karma could appear instantly or in years or even lifetimes. If you are disciplined and committed to serving humanity, you will be freed of bad karma. Its effects will be obliterated or softened/postponed.

Potential disasters in an individual's life can be deferred or even averted. The more you serve, the more blessings you will receive. Think about yourself. Evaluate every aspect of your life. Some parts of your life are clearly blessed, others may not be. Correct your mistakes. Offer pure service to transform your life. It should be obvious that I believe deeply in reincarnation from my experience and my open spiritual channels. You may not believe in reincarnation and that is fine. But I am convinced that when we die, our soul goes to the universe, and later it will return. Up down, up down—every soul goes up and comes back to begin another life.

The law of karma is epitomised by this Chinese saying: "Heaven is the most fair." For example, parents who honour, respect and love their parents a great deal will generally have children who love and honour them. The converse is also true. Karma is the reason why the Golden Rule can be found in a wide range of cultures and spiritual traditions. Do unto others as you would have them do unto you, because if you give love to others, you will receive love in return. If you argue with, disrespect, abuse, or hate others, you will receive conflict, disharmony and bad treatment in return.

Spiritual blockages or bad karma are the root blockages in life. Think about your life and the lives of your loved ones and friends. Do any of them make the same mistakes or encounter the same blockages again and again in their lives, careers, or family and romantic relationships? Why are they "stuck" in the same patterns? Why do some of them have such "bad luck"? The answer is karma. If you are on a spiritual journey, you are searching for deep soul wisdom. Wisdom about karma is a key to making any spiritual journey. When you learn how to cleanse bad karma and remove spiritual blockages with your soul, mind and body, your life will be absolutely transformed.

Your Karma Empowers You

By Suresh Jindal

RECENTLY, His Holiness the Dalai Lama has observed that Hinduism and Buddhism are siblings born of the same mother. Their views of the nature of ultimate reality are similar to each other.

The Buddhist view of Shunyata is very close to those propounded by the Advaitya schools of Hinduism. It is from this that they both derive belief in karma and reincarnation. Karma very often, due to early misunderstanding of Western scholars, is understood to be passive, impotent, helpless and defeatist. This view is misleading, and is the very opposite of the real import of karma. Karma is dynamic, ever-changing, self-actualising and self-transcending. Rather than being a helpless pawn of kismet wafted about by an arbitrary God, karma allows one to recreate oneself in one's own image and aspirations. Rather than being arbitrarily moulded and slave driven by another, karma puts the responsibility of your destiny on yourself.

In traditions that believe in eternal rest, in either heaven or hell, the question as to why people are born in extreme diversity—fortune, riches, physical beauty, in the super rich countries of the West or the living hells of Africa and Siberia under totalitarianism—are not adequately answered. Except by blind faith and belief in a mysterious and inscrutable God who works in inexplicable ways that can neither be questioned nor answered, they offer no acceptable explanation. Karma literally means action, work, and activity. We act as form in a physical body; and we also act as mental continuums of the wisdom of our feeling, perception, actualisation and accomplishment, within a world view of the nature of ultimate reality. The results of these acts leave imprints that ripen into future results. Buddhism postulates four laws that govern karma:

1. Karma is definite in that good karma will yield happiness and afflicted karma will produce suffering.
2. Karma always increases. Just as multiple fruits come from a single seed, karma too multiplies. A small act of virtue blooms manifold as does a small act of meanness.
3. The results are similar to the cause. Or you cannot make silk out of a sow's ear!
4. Like the laws of energy that govern the external world, in the inner space of one's mental continuum, karmic causes once created cannot be lost or denied.

Karmic acts leave imprints (vasanas) in our mental continuums whose results will bear fruit—both bitter and nectarine—into inexorable ripening. Like a minor humiliation to another fertilises vast fields of resentment, spite and hatred, a single karmic seed gives birth to a vast tree of fruit. Like a seed of spinach will not yield a tree of guavas, an act of compassion will not produce hatred; an act of abuse will not produce love. Similar seeds will give similar fruit.

It is a universal experience that "luck" or "destiny" or "kismet" can make a sudden about-turn. Gain turns to loss, fame to disgrace, profit to loss, and happiness to sorrow in a single instance. Glowing radiant health can find itself being silently eaten by cancer or heart disease. The Buddhist view of impermanence observes that objects give the illusion of appearing solid and permanent due to dependence on various causes and conditions. They exist when the causes exist and cease when the causes cease. The causes and conditions of our physio-psychological aggregates of form, feeling, perception, volition and consciousness are results of our karmic actions. And, in turn, every act we perform every moment impacts upon the subsequent moments of our being and consciousness. All phenomena are in an intransigent state of dynamic flux, and change from moment to moment. Nothing is permanent and forever, including misery and suffering. It is possible to abandon this endless cycle of conditioned existence by one's efforts and without the intervention of some Superior Being. We ourselves create causes and conditions of our misery. And it is we alone that can get us out of it. Our acts must create those causes and conditions that can give us happiness and liberate us from suffering. By creating deserts of hatred and greed, we cannot harvest groves of love and kindness. To eliminate suffering, you have to uproot the roots of the causes and conditions of suffering. This wisdom is available to every being for, as the Shakya Muni said, every sentient is a potential Buddha. Our negative karmas obfuscate us from seeing this profound truth.

It's Karma At Work, Don't Blame God

By Parmarthi Raina

AN proposes, God disposes. This oft-quoted saying suggests that, in the ultimate, it is God who decides the outcome of our efforts at achieving our aspirations and goals. Could this be true? We talk about the injustice in this world. All around us we see the unrighteous flourish while the virtuous suffer. Often, notorious criminals get away, the innocent get punished. The indulgent remain healthy, the cautious suffer disease. The idle get rich, the industrious remain poor. These anomalies could conveniently be explained away as good and bad luck, but what about glaring inequities at birth? One infant is born with high IQ, good looks and health; another is born to rich, caring and cultured parents, while yet another is born with physical, economic and emotional disadvantages. If God is the final arbitrator of our destiny, He must be a very partial God indeed. To a believer in a just and benevolent God, such gross inequities defy explanation.

Vedic scriptures, however, contend that man's desires, ambitions and efforts are not disposed of by God; they are disposed of by man's karma, past actions. Is karma then more powerful than God? God is all-powerful; He can do anything and everything. However, normally, God does not intervene in man's material destiny and, hence, karma holds sway. God does not even judge man's karma, for karma is self-judging. God has established the law of karma under the control of maya, His external energy, and the law is precise, strict, uncompromising, relentless and thoroughly impartial. So, if there is unexplained suffering, if there is failure despite efforts at achieving success, know that it is due to one's past karma, not God's displeasure. God is not to be blamed. If there is an unexpected windfall, that, too, is the result of one's good karma at work. As you sow, so shall you reap.

Any action, good, bad or indifferent, yields corresponding fruit. Reward and punishment are portioned out according to the nature of each person's karma. Righteous action brings rich rewards and exceptionally good action takes one to heaven, swargaloka. Bad deeds result in problems, failures and miseries. Extraordinarily bad deeds result in one being born in the form of a lower species. One's existence could be filled with torment. Our actions in previous births determine the choice of our parents. Chandogya Upanishad (V.10) says, "Those who are of good conduct will enter into an elevated or superior womb, and those who are of evil conduct will be born into the womb of a dog or swine or an outcast."

No one can get anything unless he earns it. A person may accumulate enormous wealth through means fair or foul, but he will be able to use for himself only that what he deserves. In spite of thousands of books in his library, he will not be able to read any that he does not deserve. And this deserving is produced by past karma. Retribution is the guiding principle of the karma doctrine. Retribution is awarded by our karmas, not for our karmas. A true believer feels no bitterness when misfortune befalls him and he blames no one, not even God. Such an attitude should not be mistaken as fatalistic resignation, for in reality it is wholesome; it promotes acceptance of one's situation and it inspires edification. It may be argued that because everything is predestined, we have no freedom of action. It is true that man cannot escape the fruits of prarabdha karma "past karma now fructifying" but destiny does not dictate man's current behaviour. Man has the discriminative power and, limited though sufficient, freedom to act as he pleases. If, therefore, he acts according to spiritual injunctions, he can create good karmas to reap corresponding benefits in future lives. The law of karma is optimistic and progressive because it is well within one's control to improve his future both materially and spiritually. Karma is also one of the means to moksha, liberation. Karma teaches us that in the lives of humans there is an absolute natural justice that cannot be violated and it will always prevail. It would, therefore, be prudent for us to always remember that though we may be able to circumvent man-made laws, we cannot escape the law of karma.

Karma and the Fine Art of Remapping Our Memories

By Anil K Rajvanshi

ACH one of us is born with a unique genetic make-up, which provides a basic template for our general behaviour. This behaviour is further modified by our surroundings. These interactions, especially in early life, imprint powerful memories in our brain. Our mind is the total sum of our memories which govern our actions. Our actions then reinforce our memories in a feedback loop-type mechanism. Memories or sanskars, as Patanjali calls them in his Yoga Darshan, are the genesis of karma.

Karma is action embracing the whole meaning of living. We are because of our karma. Our karma or actions, good and bad, decide our future in this or the next life. The law of karma is central to Indian philosophy.

Some say that the law of karma is deterministic: you are born according to your karma, things happen to you because of your past karmas, so it is not possible for one to change one's present life. This, however, negates the whole basis of yoga which claims that one can change memories and, hence, one's life. All four systems of yoga: jnana, raja, bhakti and karma, teach us to live positively in thought, word and deed. This helps produce positive memories and, hence, good karma.

Every individual has the power to change his destiny and memories by his actions in this life. Our actions change the neural pathways in the brain and, hence, the mind, which guides us to our future course of action. We can change our memories through yogic process and cultivation of deep thought, and change our karma. Deep thought on any subject for a long time is the essence of yoga, the sanyam in Patanjali yoga. Sanyam allows memory removal or sublimation of existing memories into new ones. Thinking deeply about a subject for a long time requires tremendous processing capability of the brain and it can only be achieved if the mind gets rid of some existing memories.

Brain research show that the brain is pliable, capable of developing new neurons, neural pathways and memories. The intensity of an experience dictates the quality of memory formation. Deep thought allows a very intense experience. When we think continuously and deeply about a particular thought, tremendous processing takes place in the mind, since the brain is evaluating millions of alternatives. This processing can be thought of as a cyclonic activity, which embraces other thoughts in its wake to produce the energy to focus on a single item. This process, when continued, helps in memory sublimation.

Why are we interested in getting rid of our memories? Our lives are full of happy and sad events. They produce happy and sad memories. Unhappy memories lead to violence, hatred and more unhappiness. Wilfully removing unhappy memories helps us live a more fruitful and happy life, liberating us from the cycle of birth and death.

To remove unhappy memories, we can think continuously about happy events so that this process ultimately dissolves unhappy memories. This is much superior to merely suppressing unhappy memories, for then, negative things become irrelevant, not suppressed. If we try to suppress negative feelings and memories, they only come back with much greater force.

Three Aspects of Karma Distinguish One's Actions

By Parmarthi Raina

IN conversation, as also in spiritual parlance, we use the word "karma" rather loosely and casually. By karma we mean the cause of our destiny or simply action or work including our burden of daily activities. The actual meaning of karma, however, is much more deep and complex. In Bhagavad Gita, Krishna called it, "...mysterious to even the most intelligent and difficult to understand". He explains to Arjuna: "One who sees work in no-work and no-work in work, is indeed wise and worthy of liberation from samsara, the never-ceasing cycle of birth and death" (Gita: 4.16-18).

The process of karma starts as soon as a thought to perform an action enters one's mind. It then translates into action in the form of speech or physical activity or both. Karma is, thus, performed by the mind in thought, by the tongue in speech or by the body in action.

The Gita classifies karma under three categories—karma, vi-karma and a-karma. Karma is right action—that is in accordance with shastric injunctions, with the best of motives and with desire for some return. Karma contributes to happiness here and hereafter. Vi-karma, or wrong action, is action that is contrary to shastric injunctions or performed with the intention of doing harm to others and results in suffering in this life or in future lives. A-karma is non-action, action that does not produce any reaction and, therefore, ceases to bind one to samsara and leads one to moksha.

Karma, vi-karma and a-karma are not to be distinguished by the action itself, but by the intention or motive behind that action. For example, if one may give in charity (daana), perform austerities (tapa) or sacrifices (yagnas) with the motive of acquiring fame or favours or for adharmic purposes, these seemingly right actions would be categorised as vi-karma. On the other hand, one may steal, cheat or even kill, but with good intentions, then these karma would be considered right action; and if they are done in support of dharma, they could even fall into the category of a-karma. When Arjuna fights the Kauravas and, in the process, kills several of his friends and relatives, it is only with the motive of upholding dharma. They were a-karma. Krishna says (Gita: 5.8), "...one who is detached in action and knows that the self (atma) does not do any karma even while performing all activities, is truly in knowledge of the truth".

To achieve the highest perfection of human life—total freedom: moksha from misery—we must perform only a-karma. A-karma can be achieved in two ways: first, by performing action without desire for the fruits of that action, the fruits being dedicated to the Lord and, second, by total renunciation of all action as in the state of samadhi. However, one must be careful and not confuse non-action with laziness or escapism, as renunciation, for that would amount to being in tamas (mode of ignorance).

Lord Krishna tells Arjuna (Gita: 9.27-28): "Whatever you do, whatever you eat, whatever you offer in sacrifice, whatever you give as charity, whatever austerity you perform—do that as an offering unto Me. Thus shall you be freed from the bonds of karma bearing good and evil fruits. With the heart firmly set on renunciation, you will attain liberation (moksha) and thereby come to Me."

Decipher the Colour Code of Your Karma

By Amrit Gangar

JAINA "soul" metaphysics has an interesting colour code called lesya, a unique concept in the phenomenology of karma. The special aura of the soul can be described in terms of colour, smell, touch or taste indicating the stages of spiritual progress of a living being, whether human, animal, demonic or divine.

Lesya is determined by the adherence of karmic matter to jiva or soul, resulting from both good and bad actions. This adherence is compared to the way dust particles adhere to an oil-smeared body.

The jiva is classified according to good or bad emotions that hold sway. The salesi or lesya-prone are all those who are swayed by emotion, and the alesi are liberated beings or siddhas who no longer experience feelings, of either pain or pleasure.

Lesya, according to Sutrakritanga, is a term that signifies colour (in Sanskrit, "light" or "tint"). Jaina scholar K C Jain says: "The Ajivika expression Chalabhitiya as explained by Buddhaghosha implies the same method of classification of men in terms of six colours." Prof H Jacobi says Mahavira borrowed the idea of the six lesyas from the ajivikas and altered it to bring it into harmony with the rest of his doctrines. As hinted in Acharanga Sutra, the classification of living beings in terms of six colours could be traced back to Parsva's doctrine of six jivanikayas.

Depending on the karmic density, the colour scheme for the six lesyas include taste, smell and touch. There are variations in colour decoding by different scholars though essentially they imply the same meaning.

The black lesya, for instance, has the colour of a rain cloud, a buffalo's horn, or is a shade darker than the colour of collyrium. The blue lesya is the colour of the red-flowered blue Asoka tree. The grey lesya is the colour of the pigeon's neck or ash. The red lesya is the colour of vermilion or red lead. The yellow lesya is coloured like the orpiment or turmeric. The white lesya is the colour of a conch.

The taste of the black lesya is more bitter than that of neem leaves; that of the blue lesya is worse than that of a wild thorn, the grey lesya is sour; the red lesya is sour-sweet; the yellow lesya is sweet as honey while the white lesya tastes sweeter than sugar. The smell of the three bad lesyas is infinitely worse than that of a dead cow, dog or snake. The smell of the three good lesyas is infinitely more pleasant than that of fragrant flowers or pleasant perfumes.

The touch of the bad lesyas is worse than that of a saw, the tongue of a cow, or the leaf of the teak tree. The touch of the three good lesyas is more pleasant and softer than that of cotton, butter or the Sirisha flower.

The six tinges suggest an ascending order of purity, black being the worst and white being the best. Jainism scholar and author of Kalpa Sutra, K C Lalwani, says, "Six persons with these six tinges desire to eat the fruits of a tree. How would they behave? The person with the black tinge will cut the tree at the very root. The one with the blue tinge will chop its branches. The one with the ash tinge will cut the branch bearing the fruit for his consumption. The one with the red tinge will pluck all the fruits, ripe or not. The one with the pink tinge will pluck only the ripe fruits. The one with the white tinge will take only those ripe fruits that have dropped on the ground." Lesya, in this sense, is a subjective inclination that induces the soul to activity and imparts to jiva a certain tinge.

Dispassionate View of the Law of Karma

Discourse: Osho

HE law of karma is not a law. It is not something scientific, like the law of gravitation. It has been hoped for centuries that if you do good, you will attain good results. If you look at nature, there are laws but science has not come even close to detecting anything like the law of karma. If you simply say any action is bound to produce some reaction, it is possible to have scientific support for it. But we are hoping for much more. We are asking that a good action inevitably brings a good consequence with it, and the same with a bad action. Now, there are many things implied in this.

First, what is good? Each society defines good according to itself. What is good in one culture is bad in another. A law has to be universal. For example, if you heat water to 100 degrees centigrade, it will evaporate—in Tibet, in Russia, in America. A law has to be universal if it is scientific. If it is a law created by people themselves, by creating a Constitution, a legal system, then it has nothing to do with science and nothing to do with existence. It is applicable only within the society that creates it. You can change it—and laws do go on changing. Something what was legal yesterday is illegal today and vice versa.

The law of karma is a hope. A man wandering in darkness, groping his way, clings to anything that gives a little hope, a little light—because what you observe in life is something totally different from the law of karma. A man who is a criminal may succeed and become the president, the prime minister or vice versa.

If you are living a poor, miserable life, the law of karma says it is because in a past life you committed evil acts. If somebody is enjoying good health, money, power, you need not be jealous of him: he has done good deeds in a past life and now he is reaping the crop. He has sown the seeds in his past life.

But why is there so much distance between sowing the seeds and reaping the crop? To me, there seems to be some conspiracy in it, not a law. Because the priest cannot manage to explain why somebody is rich when everybody knows that what he is doing is evil and still he goes on becoming richer. And we know that somebody is good, but he is starving. So what good is good?

How is the priest going to explain it away? He has found a way: the law of karma. He cannot explain it here now so he makes death come in between your actions and their results; results will be after death, in the next life. But why? If you put your hand in fire now, you will be burned now.

To me, certainly each action has its result, but not somewhere far away in a future life. The action and the result are continuous, they are part of one process. When you are kind to someone, don't you feel a certain joy? There is a kind of deep satisfaction. Have you ever felt contentment when you are angry, when you hurt somebody? The law of karma is something psychological: neither legal, nor social, nor moral. Whatever you do contains in itself its consequence.

It does not matter whether you call it good or bad, because what you call it—good or bad—will depend upon your conditioning. If you really want to know what the act brings, you have to drop your psychology; then you will know the law of karma—not before that.

(Excerpted from Personality to Individuality. Courtesy: Osho International Foundation Healing Touch)

Oneness and Wellness the Energetic Way

Discourse: Sadhguru Jaggi Vasudev

WHY do you limit yourself to the physical and the logical? If your energies are kept in full flow and in proper balance, it is capable of much more than just physical health. The word "health" comes from the root word "whole". To "feel healthy" is to have a sense of wholeness within. If we are free of diseases medically, that is not health. If we feel like a complete human being in body, mind and spirit, we are really healthy. Many are medically healthy, but not healthy in the real sense because they do not experience a sense of wellness within.

To experience a sense of wholeness and oneness, it's important that your body, mind and, above all, your energy functions at a certain level of intensity within. Now, physically one may be healthy, but still feel lethargic. You don't know why things don't happen in life the way they should, both inside and outside; this is because you are not taking care of the well-being of your energy.

For every physical or psychological situation that you go through in life, there is an energy basis which, in turn, has a chemical basis. In a way, modern allopathic medicines have become just chemistry. For every problem that arises in your body, you are just trying to take some medicine, a chemical, and come to some kind of balance. If you use one chemical to bring down one aspect, or enhance another, there is also a side-effect. For this, there is an antidote; for the antidote there is another antidote, it's an endless chain. Whatever is happening on the chemistry front in your body is only controlled by the way your energies function. Because you have excess acids within, you ingest some alkaline medicine. But why do you have excessive acids? Because of the way your mind, body and, above all, energy, functions.

In yoga, when we say health, we don't look at the body or mind; we only look at energy the way it is. If your energy body is in balance and full flow, physically and mentally you will be in perfect health. This is about going to the foundations of your energy system and activating it in a proper way, building a foundational yogic practice that establishes your energy so that your body and mind are naturally fine.

No one gets to live in perfect conditions. The pressures of life, food, air, water—all these can affect us in many ways. The more our activities are in the world, the more we're exposed to many things that can throw our chemistry off-balance and create health problems. But if the energy in our system is properly cultivated and kept active, these things will not have an effect.

Life functions in many ways. Let us say you don't know anything about electricity. This hall is dark. If I tell you to just press this button and the whole hall is flooded with light, will you believe me? You will call it a miracle, isn't it, if you don't understand how electricity works?

Medical sciences tend to limit themselves to knowing the physical body. If anything happens beyond that, you think it's a miracle. I just call it another kind of science, that's all. Don't limit yourself to the physical and the logical. This life energy in you created your whole body—bones, flesh, heart, kidney and everything. Do you think it cannot create health? If your energies are kept in full flow and proper balance, it is capable of much more than just health.

Detoxify Yourself During Festival of Paryushana

By Pradip Kumar Jain

ARYUSHANA is a major 10-day Jain festival celebrated during the month of Bhadrapada. In this period, participants practise self-purification, self-criticism and self-control in order to achieve self-improvement. Devotees during these days partake of simple and frugal meals once daily and abstain from worldly vices and addictions. They rededicate themselves to practise dharma as the scriptures define it.

Jain scriptures speak loftily of the human form of the Atman. The human incarnation of the Atman is a rare privilege and should not be frittered away in the pursuit of physical pleasures and material gains. Human beings are seen as the best and the most perfect creations of the Almighty and this incarnation must be utilised by the Atman to rid itself of worldly bondage. Dharma and viveka or discretion differentiates human beings from other life forms. Viveka helps us to realise the true Self or the dharma of the Atman.

The dharma of the Atman—Dasha Lakhsyana in Jainism—is considered a prelude to attain nirvana or eternal bliss. It consists of 10 traits, which have been equated with 10 stepping stones leading towards realising this goal. Each trait is assigned one day of the Paryushana festivities.

The dharmas of the Atman are: Mardawa which means gentleness of nature or the feeling of pride. Pride leads to immodesty and impropriety of conduct and so should be shunned. Arjava means honesty and righteousness. It implies leading a life free of deceit and craftiness. Our day-to-day dealings and business should be conducted with honesty and uprightness. Satya or truthfulness is understanding and believing in the true nature and form of things. Being truthful and behaving ethically with fellow beings is what satya is all about. Shauch means cleanliness or freedom from defilement. It involves keeping the Atman free of kshayas and other vices of the world. Sanyama means practising moderation and abstinence in everyday life.

Tapa means devotional penance. Leading the life of a recluse or hermit while keeping oneself engaged in meditation and study of religion is Tapa. Tyaga is to relinquish or to give away in charity; to donate one's material possessions and wealth willingly for the welfare of the needy. Aparigraha is applying self-imposed limit for worldly possessions. Even the desire to have more wealth and material gains is kept in check through constant practice of aparigraha. Brahmacharya or celibacy means maintaining chaste, moral behaviour under all circumstances.

The last day of Paryushana is celebrated as the day of universal forgiveness. On this day, all people forgive and seek forgiveness from one another for any hurts or offences committed knowingly or unknowingly by them. The qualities or the dharmas of the Atman—forgiveness, truthfulness, morality, moderation and charity—are also the ever-needed principles of good social behaviour. These virtues act as buffers in resolving interpersonal conflicts, family feuds and communal tensions. In society, they can play a vital role in promoting communal peace and social harmony. At the individual level, observance of these dharmas can help us attain mental peace and raise the Atman to greater glory on the path of nirvana. These dharmas can pave the way for social integration and all-round prosperity.

Fasting Or Feasting, the Choice Is Yours

By Hiten Shah

FASTING has long been considered an integral part of Jainism. It plays an important role in a monk's code of conduct. Many Jains fast on a regular basis, especially during Paryushan. Fasting destroys negative karma, helps us to come to terms with our greed, and disciplines us to "eat to live" rather than "live to eat".

Fasting is becoming popular worldwide today for deep healing and detoxification. For Jains, fasting is often a very public act. The whole community comes to hear of the person who is fasting, and people regularly enquire about his health and give their blessings. The association of fasting with the ability to endure pain and suffering has meant that those who practise it are revered and respected.

Although Jain doctrine encourages individuals to undertake regular fasting throughout the year, in the week of Paryushan there is greater visibility. For the novice, it's a journey into uncharted territory. For the experienced, it will be an opportunity to continue the tradition. Fast-breaking is a big celebration, with friends and relatives. For children, this is an entertaining time as they get a chance to spoon-feed adults.

When I first started fasting as a teenager, spurred on by an enthusiastic parent, success for me was to get to the finishing line with the minimum suffering. Initially, it was a day's fast, but flushed with the triumph of success, one soon became two, and then three and four. Finally, the big one: the eight-day fast. To complete this was an achievement to boast about. It guaranteed entry into a select group.

What amazed me initially was that my body and mind could actually take such physical and mental discipline. Feelings of hunger, anxiety, lethargy and tiredness can be so overwhelming that one inevitably has to surrender to them. However, I have also experienced how, after a couple of days, the stomach packs up and closes shop as if it were going on holiday. Fasting gives our stomachs a well-deserved rest from the regular barrage of food thrown into it day after day. That's why fasting is so recuperative.

With the experience, I realise that the achievements I once considered as mine were somewhat of an illusion. (For example: was it right to be fasting and, at the same time, wondering what you would like to eat for your next meal? Was it right to be fasting and continue to be burdened by personal and professional pressures? Was it right to let lethargy and tiredness dull my personality? Was I fasting for fasting's sake, and nothing more?)

Fasting is not about achieving material goals or fighting feelings. It is about achieving spiritual goals and controlling feelings, about understanding and appreciating the influence of diet on our emotions and using the positive energy that fasting generates to reach a higher spiritual plane. Foremost, it is an inward personal journey, not a prize-winning race. We must separate public acts from private experience.

While Paryushan represents the perfect opportunity to be introduced to fasting, it should be used as a launch pad to continue the practice on a regular basis. Fasting can help us to renew ourselves and to rekindle our energy and vitality to new heights. Given the choice between fasting and feasting, there can only be one winner. Try it for yourself and experience the light.

Balance the Spiritual and the Material

By Pranav Pandya

THERE are two aspects to human life: one that relates to the physical body, the material, and the other that relates to the inner self or the soul, the spiritual. Materialism is a tendency to lead a life of worldly pleasures. Spirituality means to keep in mind the awakening of the soul even while remaining active. Material characteristics include greed, attachment towards worldly objects and people, and egoism. We generally engage our time and effort in satisfying our material requirements.

The mind is different from the rest of the senses in that it is always dissatisfied. New hopes and ambitions arise once the old ones are fulfilled. The worth and importance of a well-mannered, disciplined person is obviously more than that of an egoistic person. No circumstances or individuals can challenge a person who is dominated by ego, whereas examples of egoistic people suffering and coming to ruin can be seen all around us. The ego-less person is respected while an egoistic person is not.

The inner self or the soul is called antaratma. Looking after the soul results in eternal peace, satisfaction, bliss and acquisition of material and spiritual benefits. Here, priority is given to the soul compared to the body. Bodily requirements are kept to a minimum and the principle of "simple living and high thinking" is adopted. This means a person who takes care of his soul has to practise restraint over the senses and remain satisfied with minimum resources.

If, for example, a person's food intake is kept low, it has the double benefit of enabling longevity and protection from diseases. The consumption of too much sugar, salt and fat can lead to diabetes, high blood pressure and arteriosclerosis, respectively. An excess usage of other senses also causes problems. For example, watching too much television or too much exposure to computers damages eyesight. Listening to loud music affects hearing. Overindulgence in sexual activities is unhealthy.

People who practise restraint experience neither financial crisis nor do they remain in debt. They maintain a healthy body and healthy mind. They are called people of character; they are respected. We should consider the whole world as family, by adopting the principle of vasudhaiva kutumbakam. Why spend valuable time and effort for the sake of a few family members only? When the feeling of vasudhaiva kutumbakam develops, a person exhibits love and compassion towards everyone and offers his services for the welfare of humanity. On the other hand, if one person or a group of persons is showered with excessive love and caring, it becomes a cause of suffering for everyone concerned.

Thinking about the welfare of the soul prevents wastage. Those who remain satisfied achieve peace. Everyone around them becomes their friend, admirer or supporter. They always remain blissful. Nothing remains to be achieved by a person who follows the path of welfare of the soul.

Relax to Overcome the Burnout Phenomenon

By Linesh Sheth

THE phenomenon called "burnout" is affecting a wide swathe of people worldwide including sportspersons, corporate executives, businessmen, students, journalists, writers and even those who feel the need to retire early because of exhaustion.

What is understood by "burnout"? It is the exhaustion produced from continuous and disproportionate strenuous work in any field. Burnout occurs when one is driven by compulsion to achieve what you are expected to achieve. You compete with yourself or with others to compensate for what you believe is lacking in your life. When it becomes a passion, you continually overwork in order to excel. Such effort consumes disproportionate amount of energy so that you burn yourself. The main reason for burnout is overspending of energy without learning to renew it on a daily basis. So, there is only one way of spending energy.

This phenomenon is increasing by the day in every field of life, perhaps because our lifestyles have become more external. Our goals are set by others rather than by our judgment of what we truly need. Again, these goals are becoming more difficult to attain while many of us are not aware how to recharge ourselves. Even role models are getting completely externally oriented where success in what we do is becoming more important than the means of achieving it.

The burnout process is reversible. The first step is to pause, review the direction of what you are doing to your body and mind and check whether you are achieving finally what you want to. Such reflection has to be authentic and should be done under guidance. The direction is neither psychological nor therapeutic in nature. It is a robust enquiry into how you want to live with respect to what you truly want in life. It is the emergence of a genuine consciousness of self-inquiry.

First, cultivate the attitude to begin to slow down and learn to relax. That, in essence, means to be available to your own self in terms of free time and to be available for certain practices that help you get in touch with your inner core. Contact with your core rejuvenates as it is the fountainhead of renewal and rebirth in every human being. I would not like to call this process as meditation but it is a simple systematic process of diving within oneself. The process is easy and effortless, has no preconditions and prior experience is not necessary.

The process involves comprehension about our present direction in life, with reference to what we truly want, learning to introspect and energise methods and practising them correctly. The crux of learning lies not in your intellectual grasp but on experiential understanding. It is good to learn from a teacher.

If we compare our body-mind with a car, we can understand the proposal easily. The car runs on a battery which is subject to two processes: operating the car functions and getting continuously recharged from within the car. If there is no recharging, the battery burns itself out. There are proven methods that harmonise our energies and recharge them through certain basic exercises. They generate flow of new energies in the most important centres of the body. It is important to learn how to remain joyful in everything we do as joyfulness in life is the antidote to burnout.

Don't Give in to Stress, Just Learn to Manage it

By Umesh Sharma

STRESS levels of students are on the rise, pressured as they are to perform superlatively in examinations. Stress is also the bane of executives who are dogged by competition and ambition. Stress-related ailments are becoming more common. Stress is different things to different people. To a mountaineer, it is the challenge of pushing physical resources to the limit by striving to achieve a demanding goal. To the motorist, it can be hassles of heavy traffic and pollution.

Stress is a major problem for many but, curiously, it is also a matter of pride in certain circles. The perception is that if you are not stressed, you are just not working hard enough. You toss and turn all night. The alarm doesn't go off. You're late for work. There's a deadline to meet, but your computer is down with virus. Three cups of coffee later, your head still throbs. Your back hurts. Your eyes sting each time you blink.

Stress is the inability to cope with a real or imagined threat to your mental, physical, emotional and spiritual well-being which results in a series of physiological responses and adaptations. It can be caused by good and bad experiences. The Upanishads say that we are a part of the world and the world is a part of us. As human beings, we live at several levels. Coping refers to our efforts to manage stressful situations.

Make a list of possible sources of stress; it will help you understand and pay attention to issues that are a source of stress. We might have a classic case of "stress overlap" when everything seems to be going wrong, all at the same time. Be aware. Take a moment to determine your main source of stress at the current time and work towards managing it.

People are often reluctant to reveal that they are stressed and will resist any suggestion that action needs to be taken. As such, stress sits in the "shadows", hidden from view. This will continue until it bursts out into the open by which time it might be either too late for remedial action or damage control becomes costly.

A further shadow can be seen when an executive chooses not to intervene in a potentially difficult situation where someone appears to be stressed. This might be because he doesn't know how to deal with it and so feels embarrassed at exposing his lack of knowledge. Alternately, he might take a "let sleeping dogs lie" approach and just hope that it will go away. Either way, the stress situation gets worse and recedes deeper into the shadows and, thus, becomes harder and costlier to address at a later date.

Everyone responds differently to stress. That is why some people seem to thrive during stressful situations while others are exhausted. Pressure is inevitable. The solution lies in active management. Pressure is a neutral force; it can be channelled for good or bad. Pressure can be the stimuli we need to enjoy our lives and learn new skills, experience excitement and get things done. It can also be the force that causes depression and anxiety, relationships breaks and even serious illness.

Resilient people accept responsibility for their life and their choices, and they understand what's gone wrong and then try to fix it. So they are able to cope with stress. Those who are not naturally resilient can learn from examples of others.

Mandala of Healing Ragas Part of Cosmic Energy

By Bindu Chawla

 EDITATION activates the intensely loving and healing properties of the cosmos, which we refer to as cosmic energy. A profound example of this healing is the raga—which happens when the musician sings it, and also when the listener listens to it—as meditation. The word raga translates as "(cosmic) love". True to its composite nature, the cosmos is said to contain 999 ragas: the "cosmic harmonies", each harmony a melodic configuration, a mandala as it were, and unique.

Even so, the gurus always say: when you practise one you practise all, when you practise all you lose all. When you sing the raga, the notes that you do not sing are also being realised in their dormant state, in the presence of their absence as it were. Each raga represents the entire cosmos, and not its fragment. Which is why the gurus will never say that such and such notes "do not" exist in a raga, but that such and such notes "are not used".

Ustad Amir Khan Saheb of the Indore gharana innovated a style that emerged from the horizontal (a rarity) and not the vertical (the usual) notescapes of the mind, resulting in cyclical, not linear, movements of the raga. In a sense, he made a novel interpretation of the vision of the Greek mathematician, Pythagoras, who gave us the concept of the eighth note, which came to be assimilated into Hindustani music. A concept that, when put to use, opened the "third eye" of the raga. For when the seven-note scale became an octave, it came to be divided into two halves, which further facilitated the yin (dark) and yang (light) theories of vaad and samvaad, of speaking and answering in music.

Ustad Amir Khan Saheb realised that it was the yang—the vaad or speaking notes—which formed the nucleus of the raga, or where its protein lay. All composing in the raga lay in its first half, where the play of notes in their twos and threes and their fours created rich musical ideas. Onward of four (five, six and so on), the music that emerged was of a repetitive nature. Ustad Amir Khan's disciple Pandit Amarnath once inadvertently let out this secret as he spoke in the middle of a performance: "Hindustani raga aadha seekhne ki zaroorat hoti hai." (You need to learn only half the Hindustani raga.)

But this is only half the story. Ustad Amir Khan Saheb combined the first half of the madhya or the middle register with the second half of the mandra or lower register—next to it—to get a double "yang" octave, handling the mandra from the perspective of the madhya. "The mandra singing became a mirror to the madhya", explained Pandit Amarnath, "rather than a repetition, encouraging intense introspection and reflectivity". As a result, the style came to be called one of the most serious (gambhir) and peaceful (chaendar) ever heard in Hindustani khayal music, which did not scream from the rooftops to make its presence felt.

What the Ustad had done was to give the raga an abstract, aural body, which is why his music is one of the most haunting from amongst the legion of artistes gone by. He had found a great way to unfold the mystic healing energies of the cosmos.

Preoccupation With Hurt Halts Healing Process

By Christopher Mendonca

To what extent is external reality conditioned by our perception of it? We often view events and respond to them in as much as they affect us; quite often not as they actually are. So many of us tend to go to pieces in search of peace, trying to exorcise ghosts we fear and which paralyse our thinking. Steeped in our woundedness, life becomes an exercise in self-protection. We do not want to get hurt.

The ancients tell the story of a distressed person who came to the holy one for help. "Do you really want a cure?" the holy one asked. "If I did not, would I bother to come to you?" "Oh yes", the master said: "Most people do." And the disciple said incredulously: "But what for, then?" And the holy one answered, "Well, not for a cure. That's painful. They come for relief."

We often think we have got rid of the disease when the symptoms cease to manifest themselves. But this is often not the case. So, peace becomes the absence of war and hangs perilously by a slender thread of anxiety that keeps us on tenterhooks, always on the lookout for a miscreant who is ready to spark off a chain of violent responses and destroy what we thought was a negotiated settlement, because the wound hasn't really healed. We think we have got rid of our anger because we have learned to "function effectively" while we unknowingly let the anger spread and destroy us from within. Functional relationships often mask a bitterness that unexpectedly blows up in our faces like an accident that has been waiting to happen. As long as we are preoccupied with our hurt, we hinder the process of healing. It does not occur to us that our hurt is a defence mechanism of the ego asking for protection because its existence is threatened.

The Kingdom of Peace, which Jesus promises, invites us to make a paradigm shift from merely seeking relief to wanting to be cured. When Jesus said that the Kingdom was within, He referred to those who had already made this shift. Sinners and tax collectors would gain entrance into the Kingdom before the self-righteous. "Blind? If you were, you would not be guilty. But since you say 'we see', your guilt remains." Herod seeks relief from the pain of his insecurity, and only succeeds in unleashing a reign of terror and violence.

Suffering that is not transformed, is suffering transmitted. On the other hand, the shepherds and the wise men, free from inner pain and anxiety of ego, experience the peace that healing brings. It is the Kingdom of God within them that allows them to recognise the Kingdom among us. For the Kingdom to be among us, the first requisite is that it be within us. It is not characterised by uniformity but rather by the experience of a union with the Ground of our Being that holds all things together in unity.

Communion precedes community. Mary, Joseph, the shepherds and the wise men are a community of worshippers because they are first in communion with God. In the birth of Jesus, they experienced complete egolessness, the total emptying of self by one who did not think that equality with God was something to be clung to. The sound of complete emptiness found an echo in their hearts empty of desire, free from pain. In this, they become the "sacrament of community", which experiences the Kingdom of God "among" us in as much as the Kingdom of God is "within" us.

Surya the Sun God, Eternal Healer

By Sudhanshu Ranjan

ING Hieron asked Archimedes to invent new weapons when the Romans were threatening to invade his native city, Syracuse. On discovering that a Roman fleet had set sail under Marcellus, the feared Roman Commander, Archimedes, turned to the king and said, "I believe I can destroy the fleet." "By what means?" asked the king. "By means of a burning mirror," replied Archimedes.

Archimedes trained a battery of specially constructed concave mirrors, that reflected the blazing rays of the Sun, directly onto the ships. And lo and behold, the fleet was destroyed!

The legendary Marcellus, on seeing the devastation wrought upon his fleet, is said to have exclaimed: "Let us stop fighting this geometrical monster, who uses our ships like cups to ladle water from the sea, and has whipped our most efficient engines and driven them off in disgrace, and with uncanny jugglery of his mind, has out-rivalled the exploits of the hundred-handed giants of mythology."

Its devastating power is only one manifestation of the Sun's awesome energy. Its true manifestation is in the form of life force. The Sun is inextricably linked with life on earth. Without it, life is impossible. Sunshine is most cherished where it is cold most of the time. In fact, people start talking of annihilation if the Sun is not visible for a few days at a stretch.

The Hindu scriptures present the Sun as the most potent god. There are only five Puranic gods and the Sun is one of them but the images of the remaining four gods—Vishnu, Shiva, Ganesh and Durga—are also found in Him. In Surya Sahastranam, several synonyms of the Sun are actually Vishnu's names and at one place He is also called Jyotirlinga, representing Shiva. Mahakal is both the name of Shiva and the Sun. Ganesha, the son of Shiva, is also represented in the Sun. Image of the rising Sun in a water reservoir or pond appears like an elephant's trunk due to the ripples, resembling Ganesha. Gayatri and Savitri are forms of the Sun. Aditya is derived from Aditi, which is the name of Durga. The worship of the Sun God means the worship of all the five Puranic gods and goddess.

Hymns of Rig Veda confirm that the Sun is the manifestation of the whole universe. Prayers to the Sun God are found in all the four Vedas unlike the names of Vishnu, Shiva, Ganesha and Durga. Vishnu does not figure anywhere in Rig Veda. Puranic gods are evolved forms of Vedic gods. The Sun is the most visible god who can be worshipped directly without a priest or intermediary. In Chhandogya Upanishad, the Sun has been called Omkar and Udgeet. Rig Veda says the Sun is the soul of the universe and controls the animate as well as the inanimate.

The Sun's rays have the amazing power to heal. Sun worship helped Sambha, Krishna's grandson, get cured of leprosy. Solar treatment was a well-developed science in ancient times. Its exponents could revive dead persons by concentrating the Sun's rays on the dead body. Till recently, Swami Viryananda, Swami Dayananda's preceptor, and Swami Vishuddhananda were experts of this science and, reportedly, could perform such miracles. Gopinath Kaviraj has recorded that he saw Vishuddhananda reviving a dead bird thus. When Alan Leo, the renowned astrologer, visited India, he was astounded to see the longevity of rural women who ate very little nutritious food. Then he noticed that they wore heavy silver ornaments and concluded that they got solar energy through the silver which probably prolonged their lives.

T'ai Chi Is the Difference Between Life and Death

By Sensei Sandeep Desai

'AI Chi can reinstate the flow of chi. Put simply, chi is that which gives life. In terms of the body, chi is that which differentiates a corpse from a live human being. To use a Biblical reference, it is that which God breathed into the dust to produce Adam. It is the life-energy people try desperately to hold on to when they think they are dying. A strong life force makes a human being totally alive, alert, and present; a weak life force results in sluggishness and fatigue. A strong man is one with strong lungs and a weak man is one with weak lungs, according to a Chinese saying.

The concept of "life force" is found in most ancient cultures of the world. It is particularly evident in Chinese, Japanese and Korean culture, where the world is perceived not purely in terms of physical matter, but also in terms of invisible energy. In India, it is called prana; in China chi; and in Japan ki. In some Native American tribes it is called the Great Spirit. For all these cultures, and others as well, the idea of a life force is central to their forms of medicine and healing. For example, acupuncture is based on balancing and enhancing chi to bring the body into a state of health. At its highest level, acupuncture involves injecting chi at just the right time and place and in the right amount to reinstate its natural flow in the patient. Energy can be increased in a human being. Consequently, the development of chi can make an ill person robust or a weak person vibrant; it can enhance one's mental capacity too.

The concept of chi extends beyond the physical body to the subtle energies that activate all human functions, including emotions and thought. Unbalanced chi causes you to become emotionally agitated and distressed. Balanced chi causes your emotions to become smooth and more satisfying. From the perspective of thought, when your mental chi becomes more refined, it enhances your creativity at all levels, including in art, business, relationships and child-rearing. Spiritual chi makes it more possible for us to enter into higher states of consciousness which lie at the heart of religious experience.

Chi embodies antithetical qualities: it can be used for healing, or it can be used for breaking stones. T'ai Chi and other forms of Taoist martial and healing arts, help you develop subtle chi-energy. In the T'ai Chi form, the mind initiates the flow of chi, which, in turn, initiates each movement. However, each movement intensifies the chi. Thus, there is a synergistic effect that greatly escalates the flow of chi over time.

    Many of us become slightly nervous when we encounter someone who seems to possess more talent than we do, but in the end it's the energy that prevails. Talent is the raw material of progress, but I doubt if it makes life any richer in the absence of energy. Those who have won fame and fortune through talent are those who devoted every ounce of energy they could summon to putting it into operation. My formula is: energy plus talent and you are king; energy and no talent and you are a prince; talent and no energy and you are a pauper.